The **BOOK**

The BOOK

ON THE TABOO AGAINST KNOWING WHO YOU ARE

ALAN WATTS

Vintage Books
A Division of Random House, Inc. New York

VINTAGE BOOKS EDITION, AUGUST 1989

Copyright © 1966 by Alan Watts
All rights reserved under International and Pan-American
Copyright Conventions. Published in the United States by
Random House, Inc., New York, and simultaneously in Canada
by Random House of Canada Limited, Toronto.
Originally published by Pantheon Books, a division of
Random House, Inc., in 1966.

Library of Congress Cataloging in Publication Data

Watts, Alan Wilson, 1915–
The book: on the taboo against knowing who you are.

Bibliography: p.
I. Self.   2. Self-knowledge, Theory of.
I. Title.
[BD450.W3   1972]   128′.3   72-4715
ISBN 0-679-72300-5(pbk.)

The author is grateful to the following for permission to quote:
Cambridge University Press for *The Nature of the Physical World*
by Sir Arthur Eddington and *My View of the World* by
Erwin Schrödinger.
Prentice-Hall, Inc., for *Quantum Theory* by David Bohm.
Copyright 1951 by Prentice-Hall, Inc.
E. J. Brill Ltd. for *The Gospel According to Thomas,* translated by
A. Guillaumont and others.
New Directions Publishing Corp. for *Collected Poems of Dylan
Thomas.* Copyright 1953 by Dylan Thomas. © Copyright 1957
by New Directions.
Dodd, Mead and Company, Methuen and Co., Ltd. and Miss D.
E. Collins for *The Collected Poems of G. K. Chesterton.* Copyright
1932 by Dodd, Mead & Company, Inc.

BOOK DESIGN BY WENDY KASSNER

Manufactured in the United States of America

9F

TO MY CHILDREN AND GRANDCHILDREN
Joan, David, Elizabeth, Christopher
Tia, Mark, Richard, Lila, Diane
Ann, Myra, Michael

CONTENTS

PREFACE

This book explores an unrecognized but mighty taboo—our tacit conspiracy to ignore who, or what, we really are. Briefly, the thesis is that the prevalent sensation of oneself as a separate ego enclosed in a bag of skin is a hallucination which accords neither with Western science nor with the experimental philosophy-religions of the East—in particular the central and germinal Vedanta philosophy of Hinduism. This hallucination underlies the misuse of technology for the violent subjugation of man's natural environment and, consequently, its eventual destruction.

We are therefore in urgent need of a sense of our own existence which is in accord with the physical facts and which overcomes our feeling of alienation from the universe. For this purpose I have drawn on the insights of Vedanta, stating them, however, in a completely modern and Western style—so that this volume makes no attempt to be a textbook on or introduction to Vendanta in the ordinary sense. It is rather a cross-fertilization of Western science with an Eastern intuition.

Particular thanks are due my wife, Mary Jane, for her careful editorial work and her comments on the manuscript. Gratitude is also due the Bollingen Foundation for its support of a project which included the writing of this book.

Sausalito, California   ALAN WATTS
January 1966

The BOOK

One

INSIDE INFORMATION

*J*ust what should a young man or woman know in order to be "in the know"? Is there, in other words, some inside information, some special taboo, some real lowdown on life and existence that most parents and teachers either don't know or won't tell?

In Japan it was once customary to give young people about to be married a "pillow book." This was a small volume of wood-block prints, often colored, showing all the details of sexual intercourse. It wasn't just that, as the Chinese say, "one picture is worth ten thousand words." It was also that it spared parents the embarrassment of explaining these intimate matters face-to-face. But today in the West you can get such information

at any newstand. Sex is no longer a serious taboo.
Teenagers sometimes know more about it than adults.

But if sex is no longer the big taboo, what is? For
there is always *something* taboo, something repressed,
unadmitted, or just glimpsed quickly out of the corner
of one's eye because a direct look is too unsettling. Taboos lie within taboos, like the skins of an onion. What,
then, would be The Book which fathers might slip to
their sons and mothers to their daughters, without ever
admitting it openly?

In some circles there is a strong taboo on religion,
even in circles where people go to church or read the
Bible. Here, religion is one's own private business. It is
bad form or uncool to talk or argue about it, and very
bad indeed to make a big show of piety. Yet when you
get in on the inside of almost any standard-brand religion, you wonder what on earth the hush was about.
Surely The Book I have in mind wouldn't be the Bible,
"the Good Book"—that fascinating anthology of ancient wisdom, history, and fable which has for so long
been treated as a Sacred Cow that it might well be
locked up for a century or two so that men could hear
it again with clean ears. There are indeed secrets in the
Bible, and some very subversive ones, but they are all
so muffled up in complications, in archaic symbols and
ways of thinking, that Christianity has become incred-
ibly difficult to explain to a modern person. That is,
unless you are content to water it down to being good
and trying to imitate Jesus, but no one ever explains
just *how* to do that. To do it you must have a particular
power from God known as "grace," but all that we
really know about grace is that some get it and some
don't.

The standard-brand religions, whether Jewish, Christian, Mohammedan, Hindu, or Buddhist, are—as now practiced—like exhausted mines: very hard to dig. With some exceptions not too easily found, their ideas about man and the world, their imagery, their rites, and their notions of the good life don't seem to fit in with the universe as we now know it, or with a human world that is changing so rapidly that much of what one learns in school is already obsolete on graduation day.

The Book I am thinking about would not be religious in the usual sense, but it would have to discuss many things with which religions have been concerned—the universe and man's place in it, the mysterious center of experience which we call "I myself," the problems of life and love, pain and death, and the whole question of whether existence has meaning in *any* sense of the word. For there is a growing apprehension that existence is a rat-race in a trap: living organisms, including people, are merely tubes which put things in at one end and let them out at the other, which both keeps them doing it and in the long run wears them out. So to keep the farce going, the tubes find ways of making new tubes, which also put things in at one end and let them out at the other. At the input end they even develop ganglia of nerves called brains, with eyes and ears, so that they can more easily scrounge around for things to swallow. As and when they get enough to eat, they use up their surplus energy by wiggling in complicated patterns, making all sorts of noises by blowing air in and out of the input hole, and gathering together in groups to fight with other groups. In time, the tubes grow such an abundance of attached appliances that they are hardly recognizable as mere tubes, and they manage to do this in a staggering variety of forms. There is a vague rule not to eat tubes of your own form, but in general there is serious competition as to who is going to be the top type of tube. All this seems marvelously futile, and yet, when you begin to think about it, it begins to be more marvelous than futile. Indeed, it seems extremely odd.

It is a special kind of enlightenment to have this feeling that the usual, the way things normally are, is odd—uncanny and highly improbable. G. K. Chesterton once said that it is one thing to be amazed at a gorgon or a griffin, creatures which do not exist; but it is quite another and much higher thing to be amazed at a rhinoceros or a giraffe, creatures which do exist and look as if they don't. This feeling of universal oddity includes a basic and intense wondering about the sense of things. Why, of all possible worlds, this colossal and apparently unnecessary multitude of galaxies in a mysteriously curved space-time continuum, these myriads of differing tube-species playing frantic games of one-upmanship, these numberless ways of "doing it" from the elegant architecture of the snow crystal or the diatom to the startling magnificence of the lyrebird or the peacock?

Ludwig Wittgenstein and other modern "logical" philosophers have tried to suppress this question by saying that it has no meaning and ought not to be asked. Most philosophical problems are to be solved by getting rid of them, by coming to the point where you see that such questions as "Why this universe?" are a kind of intellectual neurosis, a misuse of words in that the question *sounds* sensible but is actually as meaningless as asking "Where is this universe?" when the only things that are anywhere must be somewhere inside the universe. The task of philosophy is to cure people of such nonsense. Wittgenstein, as we shall see, had a point there. Nevertheless, wonder is not a disease. Wonder, and its expression in poetry and the arts, are among the most important things which seem to distinguish men from other animals, and intelligent and sensitive people from morons.

Is there, then, some kind of a lowdown on this astounding scheme of things, something that never really gets out through the usual channels for the Answer—the historic religions and philosophies? There is. It has been said again and again, but in such a fashion that we, today, in this particular civilization do not hear it. We do not realize that it is utterly subversive, not so much in the political and moral sense, as in that it turns our ordinary view of things, our common sense, inside out and upside down. It may of course have political and moral consequences, but as yet we have no clear idea of what they may be. Hitherto this inner revolution of the mind has been confined to rather isolated individuals; it has never, to my knowledge, been widely characteristic of communities or societies. It has often been thought too dangerous for that. Hence the taboo.

But the world is in an extremely dangerous situation, and serious diseases often require the risk of a dangerous cure—like the Pasteur serum for rabies. It is not that we may simply blow up the planet with nuclear bombs, strangle ourselves with overpopulation, destroy our natural resources through poor conservation, or ruin the soil and its products with improperly understood chemicals and pesticides. Beyond all these is the possibility that civilization may be a huge technological success, but through methods that most people will find baffling, frightening, and disorienting—because, for one reason alone, the methods will keep changing. It may be like playing a game in which the rules are constantly changed without ever being made clear—a game from which one cannot withdraw without suicide, and in which one can never return to an older form of the game.

But the problem of man and technics is almost always stated in the wrong way. It is said that humanity has evolved one-sidedly, growing in technical power without any comparable growth in moral integrity, or, as some would prefer to say, without comparable progress in education and rational thinking. Yet the problem is more basic. The root of the matter is the way in which we feel and conceive ourselves as human beings, our sensation of being alive, of individual existence and identity. We suffer from a hallucination, from a false and distorted sensation of our own existence as living organisms. Most of us have the sensation that "I myself" is a separate center of feeling and action, living inside and bounded by the physical body—a center which "confronts" an "external" world of people and things, making contact through the senses with a universe both alien and strange. Everyday figures of speech reflect this illusion. "I came into this world." "You must *face* reality." "The conquest of nature."

This feeling of being lonely and very temporary visitors in the universe is in flat contradiction to everything known about man (and all other living organisms) in the sciences. We do not "come into" this world; we come *out* of it, as leaves from a tree. As the ocean "waves," the universe "peoples." Every individual is an expression of the whole realm of nature, a unique action of the total universe. This fact is rarely, if ever, experienced by most individuals. Even those who know it to be true in theory do not sense or feel it, but continue to be aware of themselves as isolated "egos" inside bags of skin.

The first result of this illusion is that our attitude to the world "outside" us is largely hostile. We are forever "conquering" nature, space, mountains, deserts, bacteria, and insects instead of learning to cooperate with them in a harmonious order. In America the great symbols of this conquest are the bulldozer and the rocket—the instrument that batters the hills into flat tracts for little boxes made of ticky-tacky and the great phallic projectile that blasts the sky. (Nonetheless, we have fine architects who know how to fit houses into hills without ruining the landscape, and astronomers who know that the earth is already way out in space, and that our first need for exploring other worlds is sensitive electronic instruments which, like our eyes, will bring the most distant objects into our own brains.)[1] The hostile attitude of conquering nature ignores the basic interdependence of all things and events—that the world be-

<hr/>

[1] "I do not believe that anything really worthwhile will come out of the exploration of the slag heap that constitutes the surface of the moon. . . . Nobody should imagine that the enormous financial budget of NASA implies that astronomy is now well supported." Fred Hoyle, *Galaxies, Nuclei, and Quasars.* Harper & Row, New York, 1965.

yond the skin is actually an extension of our own bodies—and will end in destroying the very environment from which we emerge and upon which our whole life depends.

The second result of feeling that we are separate minds in an alien, and mostly stupid, universe is that we have no *common* sense, no way of making sense of the world upon which we are agreed in common. It's just my opinion against yours, and therefore the most aggressive and violent (and thus insensitive) propagandist makes the decisions. A muddle of conflicting opinions united by force of propaganda is the worst possible source of control for a powerful technology.

It might seem, then, that our need is for some genius to invent a new religion, a philosophy of life and a view of the world, that is plausible and generally acceptable for the late twentieth century, and through which every individual can feel that the world as a whole and his own life in particular have meaning. This, as history has shown repeatedly, is not enough. Religions are divisive and quarrelsome. They are a form of one-upmanship because they depend upon separating the "saved" from the "damned," the true believers from the heretics, the in-group from the out-group. Even religious liberals play the game of "we're-more-tolerant-than-you." Furthermore, as systems of doctrine, symbolism, and behavior, religions harden into institutions that must command loyalty, be defended and kept "pure," and—because all belief is fervent hope, and thus a cover-up for doubt and uncertainty—religions must make converts. The more people who agree with us, the less nagging insecurity about our position. In the end one is committed to being a Christian or a Buddhist come what may in the form of new knowledge. New and indigestible ideas have to be wangled into the religious tradition, however inconsistent with its original doctrines, so that the believer can still take his stand and assert, "I am first and foremost a follower of Christ/Mohammed/Buddha, or whomever." Irrevocable commitment to any religion is not only intellectual suicide; it is positive unfaith because it closes the mind to any new vision of the world. Faith is, above all, open-ness—an act of trust in the unknown.

An ardent Jehovah's Witness once tried to convince me that if there were a God of love, he would certainly provide mankind with a reliable and infallible textbook for the guidance of conduct. I replied that no considerate God would destroy the human mind by making it so rigid and unadaptable as to depend upon one book, the Bible, for all the answers. For the use of words, and thus of a book, is to point beyond themselves to a world of life and experience that is not mere words or even ideas. Just as money is not real, consumable wealth, books are not life. To idolize scriptures is like eating paper currency.

Therefore The Book that I would like to slip to my children would itself be slippery. It would slip them into a new domain, not of ideas alone, but of experience and feeling. It would be a temporary medicine, not a diet; a point of departure, not a perpetual point of reference. They would read it and be done with it, for if it were well and clearly written they would not have to go back to it again and again for hidden meanings or for clarification of obscure doctrines.

We do not need a new religion or a new bible. We need a new experience—a new feeling of what it is to be "I." The lowdown (which is, of course, the secret and profound view) on life is that our normal sensation of self is a hoax, or, at best, a temporary role that we are playing, or have been conned into playing—with our own tacit consent, just as every hypnotized person is basically willing to be hypnotized. The most strongly enforced of all known taboos is the taboo against knowing who or what you really are behind the mask of your apparently separate, independent, and isolated ego. I am not thinking of Freud's barbarous Id or Un-conconscious as the actual reality behind the façade of personality. Freud, as we shall see, was under the influence of a nineteenth-century fashion called "reduction-ism," a curious need to put down human culture and intelligence by calling it a fluky by-product of blind and irrational forces. They worked very hard, then, to prove that grapes can grow on thornbushes.

As is so often the way, what we have suppressed and overlooked is something startlingly obvious. The dif-ficulty is that it is *so* obvious and basic that one can hardly find the words for it. The Germans call it a *Hin-tergedanke,* an apprehension lying tacitly in the back of our minds which we cannot easily admit, even to our-selves. The sensation of "I" as a lonely and isolated center of being is so powerful and commonsensical, and so fundamental to our modes of speech and thought, to our laws and social institutions, that we cannot expe-rience selfhood except as something superficial in the scheme of the universe. I seem to be a brief light that flashes but once in all the aeons of time—a rare, complicated, and all-too-delicate organism on the fringe of biological evolution, where the wave of life bursts into individual, sparkling, and multicolored drops that gleam for a moment only to vanish forever. Under such conditioning it seems impossible and even absurd to realize that myself does not reside in the drop alone, but in the whole surge of energy which ranges from the galaxies to the nuclear fields in my body. At this level of existence "I" am immeasurably old; my forms are infinite and their comings and goings are simply the pulses or vibrations of a single and eternal flow of energy.

The difficulty in realizing this to be so is that conceptual thinking cannot grasp it. It is as if the eyes were trying to look at themselves directly, or as if one were trying to describe the color of a mirror in terms of colors reflected in the mirror. Just as sight is something more than all things seen, the foundation or "ground" of our existence and our awareness cannot be understood in terms of things that are known. We are forced, therefore, to speak of it through myth—that is, through special metaphors, analogies, and images which say what it is *like* as distinct from what it *is*. At one extreme of its meaning, "myth" is fable, falsehood, or superstition. But at another, "myth" is a useful and fruitful image by which we make sense of life in somewhat the same way that we can explain electrical forces by comparing them with the behavior of water or air. Yet "myth," in this second sense, is not to be taken literally, just as electricity is not to be confused with air or water. Thus in using myth one must take care not to confuse image with fact, which would be like climbing up the signpost instead of following the road.

Myth, then, is the form in which I try to answer when children ask me those fundamental metaphysical questions which come so readily to their minds: "Where did the world come from?" "Why did God make the world?" "Where was I before I was born?" "Where do people go when they die?" Again and again I have found that they seem to be satisfied with a simple and very ancient story, which goes something like this:

"There was never a time when the world began, because it goes round and round like a circle, and there is no place on a circle where it begins. Look at my watch, which tells the time; it goes round, and so the world repeats itself again and again. But just as the hour-hand of the watch goes up to twelve and down to six, so, too, there is day and night, waking and sleeping, living and dying, summer and winter. You can't have any one of these without the other, because you wouldn't be able to know what black is unless you had seen it side-by-side with white, or white unless side-by-side with black.

"In the same way, there are times when the world is, and times when it isn't, for if the world went on and on without rest for ever and ever, it would get horribly tired of itself. It comes and it goes. Now you see it; now you don't. So because it doesn't get tired of itself, it always comes back again after it disappears. It's like your breath: it goes in and out, in and out, and if you try to hold it in all the time you feel terrible. It's also like the game of hide-and-seek, because it's always fun to find new ways of hiding, and to seek for someone who doesn't always hide in the same place.

"God also likes to play hide-and-seek, but because there is nothing outside God, he has no one but himself to play with. But he gets over this difficulty by pretending that he is not himself. This is his way of hiding from himself. He pretends that he is you and I and all the people in the world, all the animals, all the plants, all the rocks, and all the stars. In this way he has strange and wonderful adventures, some of which are terrible and frightening. But these are just like bad dreams, for when he wakes up they will disappear.

"Now when God plays hide and pretends that he is you and I, he does it so well that it takes him a long time to remember where and how he hid himself. But that's the whole fun of it—just what he wanted to do. He doesn't want to find himself too quickly, for that would spoil the game. That is why it is so difficult for you and me to find out that we are God in disguise, pretending not to be himself. But when the game has gone on long enough, all of us will wake up, stop pretending, and remember that we are all one single Self—the God who is all that there is and who lives for ever and ever.

"Of course, you must remember that God isn't shaped like a person. People have skins and there is always something outside our skins. If there weren't, we wouldn't know the difference between what is inside and outside our bodies. But God has no skin and no shape because there isn't any outside to him. [With a sufficiently intelligent child, I illustrate this with *a* Möbius strip—a ring of paper tape twisted once in such a way that it has only one side and one edge.] The inside and the outside of God are the same. And though I have been talking about God as 'he' and not 'she,' God isn't a man or a woman. I didn't say 'it' because we usually say 'it' for things that aren't alive.

"God is the Self of the world, but you can't see God for the same reason that, without a mirror, you can't see your own eyes, and you certainly can't bite your own teeth or look inside your head. Your self is that cleverly hidden because it is God hiding.

"You may ask why God sometimes hides in the form of horrible people, or pretends to be people who suffer great disease and pain. Remember, first, that he isn't really doing this to anyone but himself. Remember, too, that in almost all the stories you enjoy there have to be bad people as well as good people, for the thrill of the tale is to find out how the good people will get the better of the bad. It's the same as when we play cards. At the beginning of the game we shuffle them all into a mess, which is like the bad things in the world, but the point of the game is to put the mess into good order, and the one who does it best is the winner. Then we shuffle the cards once more and play again, and so it goes with the world."

This story, obviously mythical in form, is not given as a *scientific* description of the way things are. Based on the analogies of games and the drama, and using that much worn-out word "God" for the Player, the story claims only to be *like* the way things are. I use it just as astronomers use the image of inflating a black balloon with white spots on it for the galaxies, to explain the expanding universe. But to most children, and many adults, the myth is at once intelligible, simple, and fascinating. By contrast, so many other mythical explanations of the world are crude, tortuous, and unintelligible. But many people think that believing in the unintelligible propositions and symbols of their religions is the test of true faith. "I believe," said Tertullian of Christianity, "because it is absurd."

People who think for themselves do not accept ideas on this kind of authority. They don't feel commanded to believe in miracles or strange doctrines as Abraham felt commanded by God to sacrifice his son Isaac. As T. George Harris put it:

> The social hierarchies of the past, where some boss above you always punished any error, conditioned men to feel a chain of harsh authority reaching all the way "up there." We don't feel this bond in today's egalitarian freedom. We don't even have, since Dr. Spock, many Jehovah-like fathers in the human family. So the average unconscious no longer learns to seek forgiveness from a wrathful God above.

But, he continues—

> Our generation knows a cold hell, solitary confinement in this life, without a God to damn or save it. Until man figures out the trap and hunts ... "the Ultimate Ground of Being," he has no reason at all for his existence. Empty, finite, he knows only that he will soon die. Since this life has no meaning, and he sees no future life, he is not really a person but a victim of self-extinction.[2]

[2]A discussion of the views of theologian Paul Tillich in "The Battle of the Bible," *Look,* Vol. XIX, No. 15. July 27, 1965. p. 19.

"The Ultimate Ground of Being" is Paul Tillich's de-contaminated term for "God" and would also do for "the Self of the world" as I put it in my story for children. But the secret which my story slips over to the child is that the Ultimate Ground of Being is *you*. Not, of course, the everyday you which the Ground is assuming, or "pretending" to be, but that inmost Self which escapes inspection because it's always the inspector. This, then, is the taboo of taboos: you're IT!

Yet in our culture this is the touchstone of insanity, the blackest of blasphemies, and the wildest of delusions. This, we believe, is the ultimate in megalomania—an inflation of the ego to complete absurdity. For though we cultivate the ego with one hand, we knock it down with the other. From generation to generation we kick the stuffing out of our children to teach them to "know their place" and to behave, think, and feel with proper modesty as befits one little ego among many. As my mother used to say, "You're not the only pebble on the beach!" Anyone in his right mind who believes that he is God should be crucified or burned at the stake, though now we take the more charitable view that no one in his right mind could believe such nonsense. Only a poor idiot could conceive himself as the omnipotent ruler of the world, and expect everyone else to fall down and worship.

But this is because we think of God as the King of the Universe, the Absolute Technocrat who personally and consciously controls every detail of his cosmos—and that is not the kind of God in my story. In fact, it isn't *my* story at all, for any student of the history of religions will know that it comes from ancient India, and is the mythical way of explaining the Vedanta philosophy. Vedanta is the teaching of the *Upanishads,* a collection of dialogues, stories, and poems, some of which go back to at least 800 B.C. Sophisticated Hindus do not think of God as a special and separate superperson who *rules* the world from above, like a monarch. Their God is "underneath" rather than "above" everything, and he (or it) *plays* the world from inside. One might say that if religion is the opium of the people, the Hindus have the inside dope. What is more, no Hindu can realize that he is God in disguise without seeing at the same time that this is true of everyone and everything else. In the Vedanta philosophy, nothing exists except God. There *seem* to be other things than God, but only because he is dreaming them up and making them his disguises to play hide-and-seek with himself. The universe of seemingly separate things is therefore real only for a while, not eternally real, for it comes and goes as the Self hides and seeks itself.

But Vedanta is much more than the idea or the belief that this is so. It is centrally and above all the *experience,* the immediate knowledge of its being so, and for this reason such a complete subversion of our ordinary way of seeing things. It turns the world inside out and outside in. Likewise, a saying attributed to Jesus runs:

> *When you make the two one, and*
> *when you make the inner as the outer*
> *and the outer as the inner and the above*
> *as the below . . .*

then shall you enter [the Kingdom]. . . .
I am the Light that is above
them all, I am the All,
the All came forth from Me and the All
attained to Me. Cleave a [piece of] wood, I
am there; lift up the stone and you will
find Me there.[3]

Today the Vedanta discipline comes down to us after centuries of involvement with all the forms, attitudes, and symbols of Hindu culture in its flowering and slow demise over nearly 2,800 years, sorely wounded by Islamic fanaticism and corrupted by British puritanism. As often set forth, Vedanta rings no bell in the West, and attracts mostly the fastidiously spiritual and diaphanous kind of people for whom incarnation in a physical body is just too disgusting to be borne.[4] But it is possible to state its essentials in a present-day idiom, and when this is done without exotic trappings, Sanskrit terminology, and excessive postures of spirituality, the message is not only clear to people with no special interest in "Oriental religions"; it is also the very jolt that we need to kick ourselves out of our isolated sensation of self.

But this must not be confused with our usual ideas of the practice of "unselfishness," which is the effort to

[3]A. Guillaumont and others (trs.), *The Gospel According to Thomas.* Harper & Row, New York, 1959, pp. 17–18, 43. A recently discovered Coptic manuscript, possibly translated from a Greek version as old as A.D. 140. The "I" and the "Me" are obvious references to the disguised Self.

[4]I said "mostly" because I am aware of some very special exceptions both here and in India.

identify with others and their needs while still under the strong illusion of being no more than a skin-contained ego. Such "unselfishness" is apt to be a highly refined egotism, comparable to the in-group which plays the game of "we're-more-tolerant-than-you." The Vedanta was not originally moralistic; it did not urge people to ape the saints without sharing their real motivations, or to ape motivations without sharing the knowledge which sparks them.

For this reason The Book I would pass to my children would contain no sermons, no shoulds and oughts. Genuine love comes from knowledge, not from a sense of duty or guilt. How would you like to be an invalid mother with a daughter who can't marry because she feels she ought to look after you, and therefore hates you? My wish would be to tell, not how things ought to be, but how they are, and how and why we ignore them as they are. You cannot teach an ego to be anything but egotistic, even though egos have the subtlest ways of pretending to be reformed. The basic thing is therefore to dispel, by experiment and experience, the illusion of oneself as a separate ego. The consequences may not be behavior along the lines of *conventional* morality. It may well be as the squares said of Jesus, "Look at him! A glutton and a drinker, a friend of tax-gatherers and sinners!"

Furthermore, on seeing through the illusion of the ego, it is impossible to think of oneself as better than, or superior to, others for having done so. In every direction there is just the one Self playing its myriad games of hide-and-seek. Birds are not *better* than the eggs from which they have broken. Indeed, it could be said that a bird is one egg's way of becoming other eggs. Egg is ego, and bird is the liberated Self. There is a Hindu myth of the Self as a divine swan which laid the egg from which the world was hatched. Thus I am not even saying that you *ought* to break out of your shell. Sometime, somehow, you (the real you, the Self) will do it anyhow, but it is not impossible that the play of the Self will be to remain unawakened in most of its human disguises, and so bring the drama of life on earth to its close in a vast explosion. Another Hindu myth says that as time goes on, life in the world gets worse and worse, until at last the destructive aspect of the Self, the god Shiva, dances a terrible dance which consumes everything in fire. There follow, says the myth, 4,320,000 years of total peace during which the Self is just itself and does not play hide. And then the game begins again, starting off as a universe of perfect splendor which begins to deteriorate only after 1,728,000 years, and every round of the game is so designed that the forces of darkness present themselves for only one third of the time, enjoying at the end a brief but quite illusory triumph.

Today we calculate the life of this planet alone in much vaster periods, but of all ancient civilizations the Hindus had the most imaginative vision of cosmic time. Yet remember, this story of the cycles of the world's appearance and disappearance is myth, not science, parable rather than prophecy. It is a way of illustrating the idea that the universe is *like* the game of hide-and-seek.

If, then, I am not saying that you *ought* to awaken from the ego-illusion and help save the world from disaster, why The Book? Why not sit back and let things take their course? Simply that it is part of "things taking their course" that I write. As a human being it is just my nature to enjoy and share philosophy. I do this in the same way that some birds are eagles and some doves, some flowers lilies and some roses. I realize, too, that the less I preach, the more likely I am to be heard.

Two

THE GAME OF BLACK-AND-WHITE

*W*hen we were taught 1, 2, 3 and A, B, C, few of us were ever told about the Game of Black-and-White. It is quite as simple, but belongs to the hushed-up side of things. Consider, first, that all your five senses are differing forms of one basic sense—something like touch. Seeing is highly sensitive touching. The eyes touch, or feel, light waves and so enable us to touch things out of reach of our hands. Similarly, the ears touch sound waves in the air, and the nose tiny particles of dust and gas. But the complex patterns and chains of neurons which constitute these senses are composed of neuron units which are capable of changing between just two states: on or off. To the central brain the individual neuron signals either *yes* or *no*—that's all. But, as we know from computers which employ binary arithmetic in which the only figures are 0 and 1, these simple elements can be formed into the most complex and marvelous patterns.

In this respect our nervous system and 0/1 computers are much like everything else, for the physical world is basically vibration. Whether we think of this vibration in terms of waves or of particles, or perhaps wavicles, we never find the crest of a wave without a trough or a particle without an interval, or space, between itself and others. In other words, there is no such thing as a half wave, or a particle all by itself without any space around it. There is no on without off, no up without down.

Although sounds of high vibration seem to be continuous, to be pure sound, they are not. Every sound is actually sound/silence, only the ear does not register this consciously when the alternation is too rapid. It appears only in, say, the lowest audible notes of an organ. Light, too, is not pure light, but light/darkness. Light pulsates in waves, with their essential up/down motion, and in some conditions the speed of light vibrations can be synchronized with other moving objects so that the latter appear to be still. This is why arc lights are not used in sawmills, for they emit light at a pulse which easily synchronizes with the speed of a buzz saw in such a way that its teeth seem to be still.

While eyes and ears actually register and respond to both the up-beat and the down-beat of these vibrations, the mind, that is to say our conscious attention, notices only the up-beat. The dark, silent, or "off" interval is ignored. It is almost a general principle that consciousness ignores intervals, and yet cannot notice any pulse of energy without them. If you put your hand on an attractive girl's knee and just leave it there, she may cease to notice it. But if you keep patting her knee, she will know you are very much there and interested. But she notices and, you hope, values the on more than the off. Nevertheless, the very things that we believe to exist are always on/offs. Ons alone and offs alone do not exist.

Many people imagine that in listening to music they hear simply a succession of tones, singly, or in clusters called chords. If that were true, as it is in the exceptional cases of tone-deaf people, they would hear no music, no melody whatsoever—only a succession of noises. Hearing melody is hearing the intervals between the tones, even though you may not realize it, and even though these particular intervals are not periods of silence but "steps" of varying length between points on the musical scale. These steps or intervals are auditory spaces, as distinct from distance-spaces between bodies or time-spaces between events.

Yet the general habit of conscious attention is, in various ways, to ignore intervals. Most people think, for example, that space is "just nothing" unless it happens to be filled with air. They are therefore puzzled when artists or architects speak of types and properties of space, and more so when astronomers and physicists speak of curved space, expanding space, finite space, or of the influence of space on light or on stars. Because of this habit of ignoring space-intervals, we do not realize that just a sound is a vibration of sound/silence, the whole universe (that is, existence) is a vibration of

solid/space. For solids and spaces go together as inseparably as insides and outsides. Space is the *relationship*
between bodies, and without it there can be neither energy nor motion.

If there were a body, just one single ball, with no
surrounding space, there would be no way of conceiving or feeling it as a ball or any other shape. If there
were nothing outside it, it would *have* no outside. It
might be God, but certainly not a body! So too, if there
were just space alone with nothing in it, it wouldn't be
space at all. For there is no space except space *between*
things, inside things, or outside things. This is why
space is the relationship between bodies.

Can we imagine one lonely body, the only ball in the
universe, in the midst of empty space? Perhaps. But this
ball would have no energy, no motion. In relation to
what could it be said to be moving? Things are said to
move only when compared with others that are relatively still, for motion is motion/stillness. So let's have
two balls, and notice that they come closer to each
other, or get further apart. Sure, there is motion now,
but which one is moving? Ball one, ball two, or both?
There is no way of deciding. All answers are equally
right and wrong. Now bring in a third ball. Balls one
and two stay the same distance apart, but ball three
approaches or retreats from them. Or does it? Balls one
and two may be moving together, towards or away
from three, or balls one and two may be approaching
three as three approaches them, so that all are in motion. How are we to decide? One answer is that because
balls one and two stay together, they are a group and
also constitute a majority. Their vote will therefore de-

cide who is moving and who is not. But if three joins them it can lick 'em, for if all three stay the same distance apart, the group as a whole cannot move. It will even be impossible for any one to say to the other two, or any two to the other one, "Why do you keep following me (us) around?" For the group as a whole will have no point of reference to know whether it is moving or not.

Note that whereas two balls alone can move only in a straight line, three balls can move within a surface, but not in three dimensions. The moment we add a fourth ball we get the third dimension of depth, and now it would seem that our fourth ball can stand apart from the other three, take an objective view of their behavior, and act as the referee. Yet, when we have added the fourth, which one is it? Any one of them can be in the third dimension with respect to the other three. This might be called a "first lesson in relativity," for the principle remains the same no matter how many balls are added and therefore applies to all celestial bodies in this universe and to all observers of their motion, wheresoever located. Any galaxy, any star, any planet, or any observer can be taken as the central point of reference, so that everything is central in relation to everything else!

Now in all this discussion, one possibility has been overlooked. Suppose that the balls don't move at all, but that the space between them moves. After all, we speak of a distance (i.e., space) increasing or decreasing as if it were a thing that could *do* something. This is the problem of the expanding universe. Are the other galaxies moving away from ours, or ours from them, or all from each other? Astronomers are trying to settle the problem by saying that space itself is expanding. But, again, who is to decide? What moves, the galaxies or the space? The fact that no decision can be reached is itself the clue to the answer: not just that *both* the galaxies *and* space are expanding (as if they were two different agents), but that something which we must clumsily call galaxies/space, or solid/space, is expanding.

The problem comes up because we ask the question in the wrong way. We supposed that solids were one thing and space quite another, or just nothing whatever. Then it appeared that space was no mere nothing, because solids couldn't do without it. But the mistake in the beginning was to think of solids and space as two different things, instead of as two aspects of the same thing. The point is that they are different but inseparable, like the front end and the rear end of a cat. Cut them apart, and the cat dies. Take away the crest of the wave, and there is no trough.

A similar solution applies to the ancient problem of cause and effect. We believe that every thing and every event must have a cause, that is, some *other* thing(s) or event(s), and that it will in its turn be the cause of other effects. So how does a cause lead to an effect? To make it much worse, if all that I think or do is a set of effects, there must be causes for all of them going back into an indefinite past. If so, I can't help what I do. I am simply a puppet pulled by strings that go back into times far beyond my vision.

Again, this is a problem which comes from asking the wrong question. Here is someone who has never seen a cat. He is looking through a narrow slit in a fence, and, on the other side, a cat walks by. He sees first the head, then the less distinctly shaped furry trunk, and then the tail. Extraordinary! The cat turns round and walks back, and again he sees the head, and a little later the tail. This sequence begins to look like something regular and reliable. Yet again, the cat turns round, and he witnesses the same regular sequence: first the head, and later the tail. Thereupon he reasons that the event *head* is the invariable and necessary cause of the event *tail,* which is the head's effect. This absurd and confusing gobbledygook comes from his failure to see that head and tail go together; they are all one cat.

The cat wasn't born as a head which, sometime later, caused a tail; it was born all of a piece, a head-tailed cat. Our observer's trouble was that he was watching it through a narrow slit, and couldn't see the whole cat at once.

The narrow slit in the fence is much like the way in which we look at life by conscious attention, for when we attend to something we ignore everything else. Attention is narrowed perception. It is a way of looking at life bit by bit, using memory to string the bits together—as when examining a dark room with a flashlight having a very narrow beam. Perception thus narrowed has the advantage of being sharp and bright, but it has to focus on one area of the world after another, and one feature after another. And where there are no features, only space or uniform surfaces, it somehow gets bored and searches about for more features. Attention is therefore something like a scanning mechanism in radar or television, and Norbert Wiener and his colleagues found some evidence that there is a similar process in the brain.

But a scanning process that observes the world bit by bit soon persuades its user that the world *is* a great collection of bits, and these he calls separate things or events. We often say that you can only think of one thing at a time. The truth is that in looking at the world bit by bit we convince ourselves that it consists of separate things, and so give ourselves the problem of how these things are connected and how they cause and effect each other. The problem would never have arisen if we had been aware that it was just our way of looking at the world which had chopped it up into separate bits, things, events, causes, and effects. We do not see that the world is all of a piece like the head-tailed cat.

We also speak of attention as *noticing.* To notice is to select, to regard some bits of perception, or some features of the world, as more noteworthy, more significant, than others. To these we attend, and the rest we ignore—for which reason conscious attention is at the same time *ignore*-ance (i.e., ignorance) despite the fact that it gives us a vividly clear picture of whatever we choose to notice. Physically, we see, hear, smell, taste, and touch innumerable features that we never notice. You can drive thirty miles, talking all the time to a friend. What you noticed, and remembered, was the conversation, but somehow you responded to the road, the other cars, the traffic lights, and heaven knows what else, without really noticing, or focussing your mental spotlight upon them. So too, you can talk to someone at a party without remembering, for immediate recall, what clothes he or she was wearing, because they were not noteworthy or significant to you. Yet certainly your eyes and nerves responded to those clothes. You saw, but did not really look.

It seems that we notice through a double process in which the first factor is a choice of what is interesting or important. The second factor, working simultaneously with the first, is that we need a notation for almost anything that can be noticed. Notation is a system of symbols—words, numbers, signs, simple images (like squares and triangles), musical notes, letters, ideographs (as in Chinese), and scales for dividing and distinguishing variations of color or of tones. Such symbols enable us to classify our bits of perception. They are the labels on the pigeonholes into which memory sorts them, but it is most difficult to notice any bit for which there is no label. Eskimos have five words for different kinds of snow, because they live with it and it is important to them. But the Aztec language has but one word for snow, rain, and hail.

What governs what we choose to notice? The first (which we shall have to qualify later) is whatever seems advantageous or disadvantageous for our survival, our social status, and the security of our egos. The second, again working simultaneously with the first, is the pattern and the logic of all the notation symbols which we have learned from others, from our society and our culture. It is hard indeed to notice anything for which the languages available to us (whether verbal, mathematical, or musical) have no description. This is why we borrow words from foreign languages. There is no English word for a type of feeling which the Japanese call *yugen,* and we can only understand by opening our minds to situations in which Japanese people use the word.[1]

There must then be numberless features and dimensions of the world to which our senses respond without our conscious attention, let alone vibrations (such as cosmic rays) having wave-lengths to which our senses are not tuned at all. To perceive all vibrations at once would be pandemonium, as when someone slams down all the keys of the piano at the same time. But there are two ignored factors which can very well come into our awareness, and our ignorance of them is the mainstay of the ego-illusion and of the failure to know that we are each the one Self in disguise.

The first is not realizing that so-called opposites, such as light and darkness, sound and silence, solid and space, on and off, inside and outside, appearing and disappearing, cause and effect, are poles or aspects of the same thing. But we have no word for that thing, save such vague concepts as Existence, Being, God, or the Ultimate Ground of Being. For the most part these remain nebulous ideas without becoming vivid feelings or experiences.

The second, closely related, is that we are so absorbed in conscious attention, so convinced that this narrowed kind of perception is not only the real way of seeing the world, but also the very basic sensation of oneself

---

[1]"To watch the sun sink behind a flower-clad hill, to wander on and on in a huge forest without thought of return, to stand upon the shore and gaze after a boat that disappears behind distant islands, to contemplate the flight of wild geese seen and lost among the clouds." (Seami) All these are *yugen*, but what have they in common?

as a conscious being, that we are fully hypnotized by its disjointed vision of the universe. We really feel that this world is indeed an assemblage of separate things that have somehow come together or, perhaps, fallen apart, and that we are each only one of them. We see them all alone—born alone, dying alone—maybe as bits and fragments of a universal whole, or expendable parts of a big machine. Rarely do we see all so-called things and events "going together," like the head and tail of the cat, or as the tones and inflections—rising and falling, coming and going—of a single singing voice.

In other words, we do not play the Game of Black-and-White—the universal game of up/down, on/off, solid/space, and each/all. Instead, we play the game of Black-versus-White or, more usually, White-versus-Black. For, especially when rates of vibration are slow as with day and night or life and death, we are forced to be aware of the black or negative aspect of the world. Then, not realizing the inseparability of the positive and negative poles of the rhythm, we are afraid that Black may win the game. But the game, "White *must* win" is no longer a game. It is a fight—a fight haunted by a sense of chronic frustration, because we are doing something as crazy as trying to keep the mountains and get rid of the valleys.

The principal form of this fight is Life-versus-Death, the so-called battle for survival, which is supposed to be the real, serious task of all living creatures. This illusion is maintained (*a*) because the fight is temporarily successful (we go on living until we don't), and (*b*) because living requires effort and ingenuity, though this is also true of games as distinct from fights. So far as we know, animals do not live in constant anxiety about sickness and death, as we do, because they live in the present. Nevertheless, they will fight when in hunger or when attacked. We must, however, be careful of taking animals as models of "perfectly natural" behavior. If "natural" means "good" or "wise," human beings can improve on animals, though they do not always do so.

But human beings, especially in Western civilization, make death the great bogey. This has something to do with the popular Christian belief that death will be followed by the dread Last Judgment, when sinners will be consigned to the temporary horrors of Purgatory or the everlasting agony of Hell. More usual, today, is the fear that death will take us into everlasting nothingness—as if that could be some sort of experience, like being buried alive forever. No more friends, no more sunlight and birdsong, no more love or laughter, no more ocean and stars—only darkness without end.

> *Do not go gentle into that good night . . .*
> *Rage, rage against the dying of the light.*

Imagination cannot grasp simple nothingness and must therefore fill the void with fantasies, as in experiments with sensory deprivation where subjects are suspended weightlessly in sound- and light-proof rooms. When death is considered the final victory of Black over White in the deadly serious battle of "White *must* win," the fantasies which fill the void are largely ghoulish. Even our popular fantasies of Heaven are on the grim side, because the usual image of God is of a very serious and awesome Grandfather, enthroned in a colossal church—and, of course, in church one may decorously "rejoice" but not have real, rip-roaring fun.

> *O what their joy and their glory must be,*
> *Those endless Sabbaths the blessed ones see.*

Who wants to be stuck in church, wearing a surplice, and singing "Alleluia!" forever? Of course, the images are strictly symbolic, but we all know how children feel about the old-time Protestant Sabbath, and God's Good Book bound in black with its terrible typography. Intelligent Christians outgrow this bad imagery, but in childhood it has seeped into the unconscious and it continues to contaminate our feelings about death.

Individual feelings about death are conditioned by social attitudes, and it is doubtful that there is any one natural and inborn emotion connected with dying. For example, it used to be thought that childbirth *should* be painful, as a punishment for Original Sin or for having had so much fun conceiving the baby. For God had said to Eve and all her daughters, "In sorrow thou shalt bring forth children." Thus when everyone believed that in having a baby it was a woman's duty to suffer, women did their duty, and many still do. We were much surprised, therefore, to find women in "primitive" societies who could just squat down and give birth while working in the fields, bite the umbilical cord, wrap up the baby, and go their way. It wasn't that their women were tougher than ours, but just that they had a different attitude. For our own gynecologists have recently discovered that many women can be conditioned psychologically for natural and painless childbirth. The pains of labor are renamed "tensions," and the mother-to-be is given preparatory exercises in relaxing to tension and cooperating with it. Birth, they are told, is not a sickness. One goes to a hospital just in case anything should go wrong, though many *avant-garde* gynecologists will let their patients give birth at home.

Premature death may come as a result of sickness, but—like birth—death as such is not a sickness at all. It is the natural and necessary end of human life—as natural as leaves falling in the autumn. (Perpetual leaves are, as we know, made of plastic, and there may come a time when surgeons will be able to replace all our organs with plastic substitutes, so that you will achieve immortality by becoming a plastic model of yourself.) Physicians should therefore explore the possibility of treating death and its pangs as they have treated labor and its "pains."

Death is, after all, a great event. So long as it is not imminent, we cling to ourselves and our lives in chronic anxiety, however pushed into the back of the mind. But when the time comes where clinging is no longer of the least avail, the circumstances are ideal for letting go of oneself completely. When this happens, the individual is released from his ego-prison. In the normal course of events this is the golden opportunity for awakening into the knowledge that one's actual self is the Self which plays the universe—an occasion for great rejoicing. But as customs now prevail, doctors, nurses, and relatives come around with smiling masks, assuring the patient that he will soon get over it, and that next week or next month he will be back home or taking a vacation by the sea. Worse still, physicians have neither the role nor the training for handling death. The Catholic priest is in a much better position: he usually knows just how to go about it, with no fumbling or humming and hawing. But the physician is supposed to put off death at all costs—including the life savings of the patient and his family.

Ananda Coomaraswamy once said that he would rather die ten years too early than ten minutes too late—too late, and too decrepit or drugged, to seize the opportunity to let oneself go, to "lay me down with a will." "I pray," he used to say, "that death will not come and catch me unannihilate"—that is, before I have let go of myself. This is why G. I. Gurdjieff, that marvelous rascal-sage, wrote in his *All and Everything:*

> The sole means now for the saving of the beings of the planet Earth would be to implant again into their presences a new organ . . . of such properties that every one of these unfortunates during the process of existence should constantly sense and be cognizant of the inevitability of his own death as well as the death of everyone upon whom his eyes or attention rests.
>
> Only such a sensation and such a cognizance can now destroy the egoism completely crystallized in them.

As we now regard death this reads like a prescription for a nightmare. But the constant awareness of death shows the world to be as flowing and diaphanous as the filmy patterns of blue smoke in the air—that there really is nothing to clutch and no one to clutch it. This is depressing only so long as there remains a notion that there might be some way of fixing it, of putting it off just once more, or hoping that one has, or is, some kind of ego-soul that will survive bodily dissolution. (I am not saying that there *is* no personal continuity beyond death—only that believing in it keeps us in bondage.)

This is no more saying that we *ought* not to fear death than I was saying that we ought to be unselfish. Suppressing the fear of death makes it all the stronger. The point is only to know, beyond any shadow of doubt, that "I" and all other "things" now present will vanish, until this knowledge compels you to release them—to know it *now* as surely as if you had just fallen off the rim of the Grand Canyon. Indeed, you were kicked off the edge of a precipice when you were born, and it's no help to cling to the rocks falling with you. If you are afraid of death, *be* afraid. The point is to get with it, to let it take over—fear, ghosts, pains, transience, dissolution, and all. And then comes the hitherto unbelievable surprise; you don't die because you were never born. You had just forgotten who you are.

All this comes much more easily with the collaboration of friends. When we are children, our other selves, our families, friends, and teachers, do everything possible to confirm us in the illusion of separateness—to help us to be genuine fakes, which is precisely what is meant by "being a real person." For the person, from the Latin *persona,* was originally the megaphone-mouthed mask used by actors in the open-air theaters of ancient Greece and Rome, the mask through (*per*) which the sound (*sonus*) came. In death we doff the *persona,* as actors take off their masks and costumes in the green room behind the scenes. And just as their friends come behind the stage to congratulate them on the performance, so one's own friends should gather at the death–bed to help one out of one's mortal role, to applaud the show, and, even more, to celebrate with champagne or sacraments (according to taste) the great awakening of death.

There are many other ways in which the game of Black-and-White is switched into the game of "White *must* win," and, like the battle for survival, they depend upon ignoring, or screening out of consciousness, the interdependence of the two sides. In a curious way this is, of course, part of the Game of Black-and-White itself, because forgetting or ignoring their interdependence is "hide" in the game of hide-and-seek. Hide-and-seek is, in turn, the Game of Black-and-White!

By way of illustration, we can take an excursion into an aspect of science-fiction which is very rapidly becoming science-fact. Applied science may be considered as the game of order-versus-chance (or, order-versus-randomness), especially in the domain of cybernetics— the science of automatic control. By means of scientific prediction and its technical applications, we are trying to gain maximum control over our surroundings and ourselves. In medicine, communications, industrial production, transportation, finance, commerce, housing, education, psychiatry, criminology, and law we are trying to make foolproof systems, to get rid of the possibility of mistakes. The more powerful technology becomes, the more urgent the need for such controls, as in the safety precautions taken for jet aircraft, and, most interesting of all, the consultations between technicians of the Atomic Powers to be sure that no one can press the Button by mistake. The use of powerful instruments, with their vast potentialities for changing man and his environment, requires more and more legislation, licensing, and policing, and thus more and more complex procedures for inspection and keeping records. Great universities, for example, have vice-presidents in charge of relations with the government and large staffs of secretaries to keep up with the mountains of paper-work involved. At times, the paper-work, recording what has been done, seems to become more important than what it records. Students' records in the registrar's office are often kept in safes and vaults, but not so the books in the library—unless extremely rare or danger-ous. So, too, the administration building becomes the largest and most impressive structure on the campus, and faculty members find that more and more of their time for teaching and research must be devoted to com-mittee meetings and form-filling to take care of the mere mechanics of running the institution.

For the same reasons, it is ever more difficult to op-erate a small business which cannot afford to take care of the financial and legal red-tape which the simplest enterprises must now respect. The ease of communi-cation through such mass media as television, radio, books, and periodicals enables a single, articulate indi-vidual to reach millions. Yet the telephone and the post office enable a formidable fraction of those millions to talk back, which can be flattering and pleasing, except that there is no way of giving individual replies—especially when correspondents seek advice for person-al or specialized problems. Only the President or the Prime Minister or the heads of huge corporations can afford the staff and machinery to cope with so much feedback.

The speed and efficiency of transportation by superhighway and air in many ways restricts freedom of travel. It is increasingly difficult to take a walk, except in such "reservations for wanderers" as state parks. But the nearest state park to my home has, at its entrance, a fence plastered with a long line of placards saying: NO FIRES. NO DOGS. NO HUNTING. NO CAMPING. SMOKING PROHIBITED. NO HORSE-RIDING. NO SWIMMING. NO WASH-ING. (I never did get that one.) PICNICS RESTRICTED TO DESIGNATED AREAS. Miles of what used to be free-and-easy beaches are now state parks which close at 6 P.M., so that one can no longer camp there for a moonlight feast. Nor can one swim outside a hundred-yard span watched by a guard, nor venture more than a few hundred feet into the water. All in the cause of "safety first" and foolproof living.

Just try taking a stroll after dark in a nice American residential area. If you can penetrate the wire fences along the highways, and then wander along a pleasant lane, you may well be challenged from a police car: "Where are you going?" Aimless strolling is suspicious and irrational. You are probably a vagrant or burglar. You are not even walking the dog! "How much money are you carrying?" Surely, you could have afforded to take the bus and if you have little or no cash, you are clearly a bum and a nuisance. Any competent house-breaker would approach his quarry in a Cadillac.

Orderly travel now means going at the maximum speed for safety from point to point, but most reachable points are increasingly cluttered with people and parked cars, and so less worth going to see, and for similar reasons it is ever more inconvenient to do business in the centers of our great cities. Real travel requires a maximum of unscheduled wandering, for there is no other way of discovering surprises and marvels, which, as I see it, is the only good reason for not staying at home. As already suggested, fast intercommunication between points is making all points the same point. Waikiki Beach is just a mongrelized version of Atlantic City, Brighton, and Miami.

Despite the fact that more accidents happen in the home than elsewhere, increasing efficiency of communication and of controlling human behavior can, instead of liberating us into the air like birds, fix us to the ground like toadstools. All information will come in by super-realistic television and other electronic devices as yet in the planning stage or barely imagined. In one way this will enable the individual to extend himself anywhere without moving his body—even to distant regions of space. But this will be a new kind of individual—an individual with a colossal external nervous system reaching out and out into infinity. And this electronic nervous system will be so interconnected that all individuals plugged in will tend to share the same thoughts, the same feelings, and the same experiences. There may be specialized types, just as there are specialized cells and organs in our bodies. For the tendency will be for all individuals to coalesce into a single bioelectronic body.

Consider the astonishing means now being made for snooping, the devices already used in offices, factories, stores, and on various lines of communication such as the mail and the telephone. Through the transistor and miniaturization techniques, these devices become ever more invisible and ever more sensitive to faint electrical impulses. The trend of all this is towards the end of individual privacy, to an extent where it may even be impossible to conceal one's thoughts. At the end of the line, no one is left with a mind of his own: there is just a vast and complex community-mind, endowed, perhaps, with such fantastic powers of control and prediction that it will already know its own future for years and years to come.

Yet the more surely and vividly you know the future, the more it makes sense to say that you've already had it. When the outcome of a game is certain, we call it quits and begin another. This is why many people object to having their fortunes told: not that fortunetelling is mere superstition or that the predictions would be horrible, but simply that the more surely the future is known, the less surprise and the less fun in living it.

Let us indulge in one more fantasy along the same lines. Technology must attempt to keep a balance between human population and consumable resources. This will require, on the one hand, judicious birth-control, and on the other, the development of many new types of food from earth, ocean, and air, doubtless including the reconversion of excrement into nutritious substances. Yet in any system of this kind there is a gradual loss of energy. As resources dwindle, population must dwindle in proportion. If, by this time, the race feels itself to be a single mind-body, this superindividual will see itself getting smaller and smaller until the last mouth eats the last morsel. Yet it may also be that, long before that, people will be highly durable plastic replicas of people with no further need to eat. But won't this be the same thing as the death of the race, with nothing but empty plastic echoes of ourselves reverberating on through time?

To most of us living today, all these fantasies of the future seem most objectionable: the loss of privacy and freedom, the restriction of travel, and the progressive conversion of flesh and blood, wood and stone, fruit and fish, sight and sound, into plastic, synthetic, and electronic reproductions. Increasingly, the artist and musician puts himself out of business through making ever more faithful and inexpensive reproductions of his original works. Is reproduction in this sense to replace biological reproduction, through cellular fission or sexual union? In short, is the next step in evolution to be the transformation of man into nothing more than electronic patterns?

All these eventualities may seem so remote as to be unworthy of concern. Yet in so many ways they are already with us, and, as we have seen, the speed of technical and social change accelerates more than we like to admit. The popularity of science-fiction attests to a very widespread fascination with such questions, and so much science-fiction is in fact a commentary on the present, since one of the best ways of understanding what goes on today is to extend it into tomorrow. What is the difference between what *is* happening, on the one hand, and the direction of its motion, on the other? If I am flying from London to New York, I *am* moving westwards even before leaving the British coast.

The science-fiction in which we have just been indulging has, then, two important morals. The first is that if the game of order-versus-chance is to continue *as* a game, order *must not* win. As prediction and control increase, so, in proportion, the game ceases to be worth the candle. We look for a new game with an uncertain result. In other words, we have to *hide* again, perhaps in a new way, and then seek in new ways, since the two together make up the dance and the wonder of existence. Contrariwise, chance *must not* win, and probably cannot, because the order/chance polarity appears to be of the same kind as the on/off and up/down. Some astronomers believe that our universe began with an explosion that hurled all the galaxies into space, where, through negative entropy, it will dissolve forever into featureless radiation. I cannot think this way. It is, I suppose, my basic metaphysical axiom, my "leap of faith," that what happened once can always happen again. Not so much that there must be time before the first explosion and time after the final dissolution, but that time (like space) curves back on itself.

This assumption is strengthened by the second moral of these fantasies, which is the more startling. Here applies the French proverb *plus ça change, plus c'est la même chose*—the more it changes, the more it's the same thing. Change is in some sense an illusion, for *we are always at the point where any future can take us!* If the human race develops an electronic nervous system, outside the bodies of individual people, thus giving us all one mind and one global body, this is almost precisely what has happened in the organization of cells which compose our own bodies. We have already done it.

Furthermore, our bodily cells, and their smallest components, appear and disappear much as light-waves vibrate and as people go from birth to death. A human body is like a whirlpool; there seems to be a constant form, called the whirlpool, but it functions for the very reason that no water stays in it. The very molecules and atoms of the water are also "whirlpools"—patterns of motion containing no constant and irreducible "stuff." Every person is the form taken by a stream—a marvelous torrent of milk, water, bread, beefsteak, fruit, vegetables, air, light, radiation—all of which are streams in their own turn. So with our institutions. There is a "constant" called the University of California in which nothing stays put: students, faculty, administrators, and even buildings come and go, leaving the university itself only as a continuing process, a pattern of behavior.

As to powers of prediction and control, the individual organism has already accomplished these in a measure which must have astounded the neurons when they first learned the trick. And if we reproduce ourselves in terms of mechanical, plastic, and electronic patterns, this is not really new. Any evolving species must look with misgivings on those of its members who first show signs of change, and will surely regard them as dangerous or crazy. Moreover, this new and unexpected type of reproduction is surely no more weird than many of the great variety of methods already found in the biological world—the startling transformation of caterpillar into butterfly, or the arrangement between bees and flowers, or the unpleasant but marvelously complex system of the anopheles mosquito.

If all this ends with the human race leaving no more trace of itself in the universe than a system of electronic patterns, why should that trouble us? *For that is exactly what we are now!* Flesh or plastic, intelligence or mechanism, nerve or wire, biology or physics—it all seems to come down to this fabulous electronic dance, which, at the macroscopic level, presents itself to itself as the whole gamut of forms and "substances."

But the underlying problem of cybernetics, which makes it an endless success/failure, is to control the process of control itself. Power is not necessarily wisdom. I may have virtual omnipotence in the government of my body and my physical environment, but how am I to control myself so as to avoid folly and error in its use? Geneticists and neurologists may come to the point of being able to produce any type of human character to order, but how will they be able to know what types of character will be needed? The situation of a pioneer culture calls for tough and aggressive individualists, whereas urban-industrial culture requires sociable and cooperative team-workers. As social change increases in speed, how are geneticists to foresee the adaptations of taste, temperament, and motivation that will be necessary twenty or thirty years ahead? Furthermore, every act of interference with the course of nature changes it in unpredictable ways. A human organism which has absorbed antibiotics is not quite the same kind of organism that it was before, because the behavior of its micro-organisms has been significantly altered. The more one interferes, the more one must analyze an ever-growing volume of detailed information about the results of interference on a world whose infinite details are inextricably interwoven. Already this information, even in the most highly specialized sciences, is so vast that no individual has time to read it—let alone absorb it.

In solving problems, technology creates new problems, and we seem, as in *Through the Looking-Glass,* to have to keep running faster and faster to stay where we are. The question is then whether technical progress actually "gets anywhere" in the sense of increasing the delight and happiness of life. There is certainly a sense of exhilaration or relief at the moment of change—at the first few uses of telephone, radio, television, jet aircraft, miracle drug, or calculating machine. But all too soon these new contrivances are taken for granted, and we find ourselves oppressed with the new predicaments which they bring with them. A successful college president once complained to me, "I'm so busy that I'm going to have to get a helicopter!" "Well," I answered, "you'll be ahead so long as you're the only president who has one. But don't get it. Everyone will expect more out of you."

Technical progress is certainly impressive from the short-run standpoint of the individual. Speaking as an old man in the 1960s, Sir Cedric Hardwicke said that his only regret was that he could not have lived in the Victorian Age—with penicillin. I am still grateful that I do not have to submit to the doctoring and dentistry of my childhood, yet I realize that advances in one field are interlocked with advances in all others. I could not have penicillin or modern anesthesia without aviation, electronics, mass communication, superhighways, and industrial agriculture—not to mention the atomic bomb and biological warfare.

Taking, therefore, a longer and wider view of things, the entire project of "conquering nature" appears more and more of a mirage—an increase in the pace of living without fundamental change of position, just as the Red

Queen suggested. But technical progress becomes a way of stalling faster and faster because of the basic illusion that man and nature, the organism and the environment, the controller and the controlled are quite different things. We might "conquer" nature if we could first, or at the same time, conquer our own nature, though we do not see that human nature and "outside" nature are all of a piece. In the same way, we do not see that "I" as the knower and controller am the same fellow as "myself" as something to be known and controlled. The self-conscious feedback mechanism of the cortex allows us the hallucination that we are two souls in one body—a rational soul and an animal soul, a rider and a horse, a good guy with better instincts and finer feelings and a rascal with rapacious lusts and unruly passions. Hence the marvelously involved hypocrisies of guilt and penitence, and the frightful cruelties of punishment, warfare, and even self-torment in the name of taking the side of the good soul against the evil. The more it sides with itself, the more the good soul reveals its inseparable shadow, and the more it disowns its shadow, the more it becomes it.

Thus for thousands of years human history has been a magnificently futile conflict, a wonderfully staged panorama of triumphs and tragedies based on the resolute taboo against admitting that black goes with white. Nothing, perhaps, ever got nowhere with so much fascinating ado. As when Tweedledum and Tweedledee *agreed* to have a battle, the essential trick of the Game of Black-and-White is a most tacit conspiracy for the partners to conceal their unity, and to look as different as possible. It is like a stage fight so well acted that the audience is ready to believe it a real fight. Hidden behind their explicit differences is the implicit unity of what Vedanta calls the Self, the One-without-a-second, the *what* there is and the *all* that there is which conceals itself in the form of you.

If, then, there is this basic unity between self and other, individual and universe, how have our minds become so narrow that we don't know it?

Three

HOW TO BE
A GENUINE FAKE

The cat has already been let out of the bag. The inside information is that yourself as "just little me" who "came into this world" and lives temporarily in a bag of skin is a hoax and a fake. The fact is that because no one thing or feature of this universe is separable from the whole, the only real You, or Self, is the whole. The rest of this book will attempt to make this so clear that you will not only understand the words but *feel* the fact. The first step is to understand, as vividly as possible, how the hoax begins.

We must first look at the form and behavior of the hoax itself. I have long been interested in trying to find out how people experience, or sense, their own existence—for what specific sensations do they use the word "I"?

Few people seem to use the word for their whole physical organism. "I have a body" is more common than "I am a body." We speak of "my" legs as we speak of "my" clothes, and "I" seems to remain intact even if the legs are amputated. We say, "I speak, I walk, I think, and (even) I breathe." But we do not say, "I shape my bones, I grow my nails, and I circulate my blood." We seem to use "I" for something *in* the body but not really *of* the body, for much of what goes on in the body seems to happen to "I" in the same way as external events. "I" is used as the center of voluntary behavior and conscious attention, but not consistently. Breathing is only partially voluntary, and we say "I was sick" or "I dreamed" or "I fell asleep" as if the verbs were not passive but active.

Nevertheless, "I" usually refers to a center in the body, but different peoples feel it in different places. For some cultures, it is in the region of the solar plexus. The Chinese *hsin,* the heart-mind or soul, is found in the center of the chest. But most Westerners locate the ego in the head, from which center the rest of us dangles. The ego is somewhere behind the eyes and between the ears. It is as if there sat beneath the dome of the skull a controlling officer who wears earphones wired to the ears, and watches a television screen wired to the eyes. Before him stands a great panel of dials and switches connected with all other parts of the body that yield conscious information or respond to the officer's will.

This controlling officer "sees" sights, "hears" sounds,

"feels" feelings, and "has" experiences. These are common but redundant ways of talking, for seeing a sight is just seeing, hearing a sound is just hearing, feeling a feeling is just feeling, and having an experience is just experiencing. But that these redundant phrases are so commonly used shows that most people think of themselves as separate from their thoughts and experiences. All this can get marvelously complicated when we begin to wonder whether our officer has another officer inside *his* head, and so *ad infinitum!*

> There was a young man who said, "Though
> It seems that I know that I know,
>   What I would like to see
>   Is the 'I' that knows 'me'
> When I know that I know that I know."

One of the most important items in our officer's equipment is his recording and filing system—the memory which he constantly "consults" so as to know how to interpret and respond to his sensory input. Without this equipment, he could have no sensation of constancy—of being the *same* officer as he was seconds ago. Although memory records are much more fluid and elusive than photographic film or magnetic tape, the accumulation of memories is an essential part of the ego-sensation. It gives the impression of oneself, the officer, as something that remains while life goes by— as if the conscious self were a stable mirror reflecting a passing procession. This further exaggerates the feeling of separateness, of oneself changing at a pace so much slower than outside events and inside thoughts that you seem to stand aside from them as an independent observer. But memories persist as the whirlpool persists. Conscious attention seems to scan them as computers scan their ever-cycling tapes or other storage mechanisms. Memory is an enduring pattern of motion, like the whirlpool, rather than an enduring substance, like a mirror, a wax tablet, or a sheet of paper. If memories are stored in neurons, there is no standing aside from the stream of events, for neurons flow along in the same stream as events outside the skull. After all, your neurons are part of my external world, and mine of yours! All our insides are outside, there in the physical world. But, conversely, the outside world has no color, shape, weight, heat, or motion without "inside" brains. It has these qualities only *in relation* to brains, which are, in turn, members of itself.

Wherever people may feel that the ego is located, and however much, or little, of the physical body is identified with it, almost all agree that "I" am *not* anything outside my skin. As Shakespeare's King John says to Hubert, "Within this wall of flesh there is a soul counts thee her creditor." The skin is always considered as a wall, barrier, or boundary which definitively separates oneself from the world—despite the fact that it is covered with pores breathing air and with nerve-ends relaying information. The skin informs us just as much as it outforms; it is as much a bridge as a barrier. Nevertheless, it is our firm conviction that beyond this "wall of flesh" lies an alien world only slightly concerned with us, so that much energy is required to command or attract its attention, or to change its behavior. It was there before we were born, and it will continue after we die. We live in it temporarily as rather unimportant fragments, disconnected and alone.

This whole illusion has its history in ways of thinking—in the images, models, myths, and language systems which we have used for thousands of years to make sense of the world. These have had an effect on our perceptions which seems to be strictly hypnotic. It is largely by *talking* that a hypnotist produces illusions and strange behavioral changes in his subjects—talking coupled with relaxed fixation of the subject's conscious attention. The stage magician, too, performs most of his illusions by patter and misdirection of attention. Hypnotic illusions can be vividly sensuous and real to the subject, even after he has come out of the so-called "hypnotic trance."

It is, then, as if the human race had hypnotized or talked itself into the hoax of egocentricity. There is no one to blame but ourselves. We are not victims of a conspiracy arranged by an external God or some secret society of manipulators. If there is any biological foundation for the hoax it lies only in the brain's capacity for narrowed, attentive consciousness hand-in-hand with its power of recognition—of knowing about knowing and thinking about thinking with the use of images and languages. My problem as a writer, using words, is to dispel the illusions of language while employing one of the languages that generates them. I can succeed only on the principle of "a hair of the dog that bit you."

Apart from such human artifacts as buildings and roads (especially Roman and American roads), our universe, including ourselves, is thoroughly wiggly. Its features are wiggly in both shape and conduct. Clouds, mountains, plants, rivers, animals, coastlines—all wiggle. They wiggle so much and in so many different ways that no one can really make out where one wiggle begins and another ends, whether in space or in time. Some French classicist of the eighteenth century complained that the Creator had seriously fallen down on the job by failing to arrange the stars with any elegant symmetry, for they seem to be sprayed through space like the droplets from a breaking wave. Is all this one thing wiggling in many different ways, or many things wiggling on their own? Are there "things" that wiggle, or are the wigglings the same as the things? It depends upon how you figure it.

Millennia ago, some genius discovered that such wiggles as fish and rabbits could be caught in nets. Much later, some other genius thought of catching the world in a net. By itself, the world goes something like this:

But now look at this wiggle through a net:

The net has "cut" the big wiggle into little wiggles, all
contained in squares of the same size. Order has been
imposed on chaos. We can now say that the wiggle
goes so many squares to the left, so many to the right,
so many up, or so many down, and at last we have its
number. Centuries later, the same image of the net was
imposed upon the world as the lines of both celestial
and terestrial latitude and longitude, as graph paper for
plotting mathematical wiggles, as pigeonholes for filing, and as the ground plan for cities. The net has thus
become one of the presiding images of human thought.
But it is always an image, and just as no one can use
the equator to tie up a package, the real wiggly world
slips like water through our imaginary nets. However
much we divide, count, sort, or classify this wiggling

into particular things and events, this is no more than a way of thinking about the world: it is never *actually* divided.

Another powerful image is the Ceramic Model of the universe, in which we think of it as so many forms of one or more substances, as pots are forms of clay, and as God is said to have created Adam from the dust. This has been an especially troublesome image, bewildering philosophers and scientists for centuries with such idiotic questions as: "How does form (or energy) influence matter?" "What is matter?" "What happens to form (the soul) when it leaves matter (the body)?" "How is it that 'mere' matter has come to be arranged in orderly forms?" "What is the relationship between mind and body?"

Problems that remain persistently insoluble should always be suspected as questions asked in the wrong way, like the problem of cause and effect. Make a spurious division of one process into two, forget that you have done it, and then puzzle for centuries as to how the two get together. So with "form" and "matter." Because no one ever discovered a piece of formless matter, or an immaterial form, it should have been obvious that there was something wrong with the Ceramic Model. The world is no more formed out of matter than trees are "made" of wood. The world is neither form nor matter, for these are two clumsy terms for the same process, known vaguely as "the world" or "existence." Yet the illusion that every form consists of, or is made of, some kind of basic "stuff" is deeply embedded in our common sense. We have quite forgotten that both "matter" and "meter" are alike derived from the Sanskrit root *matr-,* "to measure," and that the "material" world means no more than the world as measured or measurable—by such abstract images as nets or matrices, inches, seconds, grams, and decibels. The term "material" is often used as a synonym for the word "physical," from the Greek *physis* (nature), and the original Indo-European *bheu* (to become). There is nothing in the words to suggest that the material or physical world is made of any kind of stuff according to the Ceramic Model, which must henceforth be called the Crackpot Model.

But the Crackpot Model of the world as formed of clay has troubled more than the philosophers and the scientists. It lies at the root of the two major myths which have dominated Western civilization, and these, one following upon the other, have played an essential part in forming the illusion of the "real person."

If the world is basically "mere stuff" like clay, it is hard to imagine that such inert dough can move and form itself. Energy, form, and intelligence must therefore come into the world from outside. The lump must be leavened. The world is therefore conceived as an artifact, like a jar, a statue, a table or a bell, and if it is an artifact, someone must have made it, and someone must also have been responsible for the original stuff. That, too, must have been "made." In Genesis the primordial stuff "without form, and void" is symbolized as water, and, as water does not wave without wind, nothing can happen until the Spirit of God moves upon its face. The forming and moving of matter is thus attributed to intelligent Spirit, to a conscious force or energy *informing* matter so that its various shapes come and go, live and die.

Yet in the world as we now know it, many things

are clearly wrong, and one hesitates to attribute these to the astonishing Mind capable of making this world in the beginning. We are loath to believe that cruelty, pain, and malice come directly from the Root and Ground of Being, and hope fervently that God at least is the perfection of all that we can imagine as wisdom and justice. (We need not enter, here, into the fabulous and insoluble Problem of Evil which this model of the universe creates, save to note that it arises from the model itself.) The peoples who developed this myth were ruled by patriarchs or kings, and such superkings as the Egyptian, Chaldean, and Persian monarchs suggested the image of God as the Monarch of the Universe, perfect in wisdom and justice, love and mercy, yet nonetheless stern and exacting. I am not, of course, speaking of God as conceived by the most subtle Jewish, Christian, and Islamic theologians, but of the popular image. For it is the vivid image rather than the tenuous concept which has the greater influence on common sense.

The image of God as a personal Being, somehow "outside" or other than the world, had the merit of letting us feel that life is based on intelligence, that the laws of nature are everywhere consistent in that they proceed from *one* ruler, and that we could let our imaginations go to the limit in conceiving the sublime qualities of this supreme and perfect Being. The image also gave everyone a sense of importance and meaning. For this God is directly aware of every tiniest fragment of dust and vibration of energy, since it is just his awareness of it that enables it to be. This awareness is also love and, for angels and men at least, he has planned an everlasting life of the purest bliss which is to begin at the end of mortal time. But of course there are strings attached to this reward, and those who purposely and relentlessly deny or disobey the divine will must spend eternity in agonies as intense as the bliss of good and faithful subjects.

The problem of this image of God was that it became too much of a good thing. Children working at their desks in school are almost always put off when even a kindly and respected teacher watches over their shoulders. How much more disconcerting to realize that each single deed, thought, and feeling is watched by the Teacher of teachers, that nowhere on earth or in heaven is there any hiding-place from the Eye which sees all and judges all.

To many people it was therefore an immense relief when Western thinkers began to question this image and to assert that the hypothesis of God was of no help in describing or predicting the course of nature. If *everything*, they said, was the creation and the operation of God, the statement had no more logic than "Everything is up." But, as so often happens, when one tyrant is dethroned, a worse takes his place. The Crackpot Myth was retained without the Potter. The world was still understood as an artifact, but on the model of an automatic machine. The laws of nature were still there, but no lawmaker. According to the deists, the Lord had made this machine and set it going, but then went to sleep or off on a vacation. But according to the atheists, naturalists, and agnostics, the world was *fully* automatic. It had constructed itself, though not on purpose. The stuff of matter was supposed to consist of atoms like minute billiard balls, so small as to permit no further division or analysis. Allow these atoms to wiggle around in various permutations and combinations for an indefinitely long time, and at *some* time in virtually infinite time they will fall into the arrangement that we now have as the world. The old story of the monkeys and typewriters.

In this Fully Automatic Model of the universe shape and stuff survived as energy and matter. Human beings, mind and body included, were parts of the system, and thus they were possessed of intelligence and feeling as a consequence of the same interminable gyrations of atoms. But the trouble about the monkeys with typewriters is that when at last they get around to typing the *Encyclopaedia Britannica,* they may at any moment relapse into gibberish. Therefore, if human beings want to maintain their fluky status and order, they must work with full fury to defeat the merely random processes of nature. It is most strongly emphasized in this myth that matter is brute and energy blind, that all nature outside human, and some animal, skins is a profoundly stupid and insensitive mechanism. Those who continued to believe in Someone-Up-There-Who-Cares were ridiculed as woolly-minded wishful thinkers, poor weaklings unable to face man's grim predicament in a heartless universe where survival is the sole privilege of the tough guys.

If the all-too-intelligent God was disconcerting, relief in getting rid of him was short-lived. He was replaced by the Cosmic Idiot, and people began to feel more estranged from the universe than ever. This situation merely reinforced the illusion of the loneliness and separateness of the ego (now a "mental mechanism") and people calling themselves naturalists began the biggest war on nature ever waged.

In one form or another, the myth of the Fully Automatic Model has become extremely plausible, and in some scientific and academic disciplines it is as much a sacrosanct dogma as any theological doctrine of the past—despite contrary trends in physics and biology. For there are fashions in myth, and the world-conquering West of the nineteenth century needed a philosophy of life in which *realpolitik*—victory for the tough people who face the bleak facts—was the guiding principle. Thus the bleaker the facts you face, the tougher you seem to be. So we vied with each other to make the Fully Automatic Model of the universe as bleak as possible.

Nevertheless it remains a myth, with all the positive and negative features of myth as an image used for making sense of the world. It is doubtful whether Western science and technology would have been possible unless we had tried to understand nature in terms of mechanical models. According to Joseph Needham, the Chinese—despite all their sophisitication—made little progress in science because it never occurred to them to think of nature as mechanism, as "composed" of separable parts and "obeying" logical laws. Their view of the universe was organic. It was not a game of billiards in which the balls knocked each other around in a cause-and-effect series. What were causes and effects to us were to them "correlatives"—events that arose mutually, like back and front. The "parts" of their universe were not separable, but as fully interwoven as the act of selling with the act of buying.[1]

---

[1]"Until the middle of the 17th century Chinese and European scientific theories were about on a par, and only thereafter did Eu-

A "made" universe, whether of the Crackpot or Fully Automatic Model, is made of bits, and the bits are the basic realities of nature. Nature is therefore to be understood by microscopy and analysis, to find out what the bits are and how they are put together. This was the view of the nominalist philosophers of the late Middle Ages, who strongly opposed the then-called realists for maintaining that such entities as Mankind or Human Nature were real "substances" underlying the "accidents" of particular men and women. Every individual was therefore an example or case of the human "substance," though the word as then used did not mean matter or stuff but a kind of essence standing *(stance)* under *(sub)* its particular manifestations. The nominalists maintained that this was nonsense. For them, Mankind was no more than the sum total of individual people. Mankind was not a substance but simply a name for a class of creatures; it was not real but merely nominal.

Nominalism, as we know, became the dominant attitude of Western thought and especially of the philosophy of science. In the eighteenth century Rousseau went so far as to suggest that Society and the State had

ropean thought begin to move ahead so rapidly. But though it marched under the banner of Cartesian-Newtonian mechanicism, that viewpoint could not permanently suffice for the needs of science—the time came when it was imperative to look upon physics as the study of the smaller organisms, and biology as the study of the larger organisms. When the time came, Europe (or rather, by then, the world) was able to draw up a mode of thinking very old, very wise, and not characteristically European at all." Needham, *Science and Civilisation in China.* Cambridge University Press, 1956. Vol. II, p. 303.

originally been formed by a contract between individuals. Society was an association, like the Rotary Club, which individuals had at some time joined and thereby abandoned their original independence. But from the standpoint of modern sociology we feel that man is necessarily a social thing, if only for the reason that no individual can come into being without a father and a mother—and this is already society. Until quite recent times it has been the prevailing view of Western science that animals and plants, rocks and gases, are "composed" of such units as molecules, cells, atoms, and other particles in much the same way that a house is composed of bricks.

But a consistent nominalist will have to be forced into the position that there really is no such thing as the human body: there are only the particular molecules of which it is composed, or only the particular atoms— not to mention electrons, protons, neutrons, and so forth. Obviously, these particles do not by themselves constitute the human body. The whole is greater than the sum of its parts if only for the fact that a scientific description of the body must take account of the order or pattern in which the particles are arranged and of what they are doing.

> The man behind the microscope
> Has this advice for you:
> "Instead of asking what it is,
> Just ask, 'what does it do?' "

But even this is not enough. We must also ask, "In what surroundings is it doing it?" If a description of the human body must include the description of what it, and all its "parts," are *doing*—that is, of its *behavior*—this behavior will be one thing in the open air but quite another in a vacuum, in a furnace, or under water. Blood in a test-tube is not the same thing as blood in the veins because it is not behaving in the same way. Its behavior has changed because its environment or context has changed, just as the meaning of one and the same word may change according to the kind of sentence in which it is used. There is a vast difference between the bark of a tree and the bark of a dog.

It is not enough, therefore, to describe, define, and try to understand things or events by analysis alone, by taking them to pieces to find out "how they are made." This tells us much, but probably rather less than half the story. Today, scientists are more and more aware that what things are, and what they are doing, depends on where and when they are doing it. If, then, the definition of a thing or event must include definition of its environment, we realize that any given thing *goes with* a given environment so intimately and inseparably that it is more difficult to draw a clear boundary between the thing and its surroundings.

This was the grain of truth in the primitive and unreliable science of astrology—as there were also grains of truth in alchemy, herbal medicine, and other primitive sciences. For when the astrologer draws a picture of a person's character or soul, he draws a hororscope—that is, a very rough and incomplete picture of the whole universe as it stood at the moment of that person's birth. But this is at the same time a vivid way of saying that your soul, or rather your essential Self, is the whole cosmos as it is centered around the particular time, place, and activity called John Doe. Thus the soul is not in the body, but the body in the soul, and the soul is the entire network of relationships and processes which make up your environment, and apart from which you are nothing. A scientific astrology, if it could ever be worked out, would have to be a thorough description of the individual's total environment—social, biological, botanical, meteorological, and astronomical—throughout every moment of his life.

But as things are, we define (and so come to feel) the individual in the light of our narrowed "spotlight" consciousness which largely ignores the field or environment in which he is found. "Individual" is the Latin form of the Greek "atom"—that which cannot be cut or divided any further into separate parts. We cannot chop off a person's head or remove his heart without killing him. But we can kill him just as effectively by separating him from his proper environment. This implies that the only true atom is the universe—that total system of interdependent "thing-events" which can be separated from each other only in name. For the human individual is not built as a car is built. He does not come into being by assembling parts, by screwing a head onto a neck, by wiring a brain to a set of lungs, or by welding veins to a heart. Head, neck, heart, lungs, brain, veins, muscles, and glands are separate names but not separate events, and these events grow into being simultaneously and interdependently. In precisely the same way, the individual is separate from his universal environment only in name. When this is not recognized, you have been fooled by your name. Confusing names with nature, you come to believe that having a

separate name makes you a separate being. This is—
rather literally—to be spellbound.

Naturally, it isn't the mere fact of being named that
brings about the hoax of being a "real person"; it is all
that goes with it. The child is tricked into the ego-
feeling by the attitudes, words, and actions of the society which surrounds him—his parents, relatives,
teachers, and, above all, his similarly hoodwinked peers.
Other people teach us who we are. Their attitudes to
us are the mirror in which we learn to see ourselves,
but the mirror is distorted. We are, perhaps, rather
dimly aware of the immense power of our social environment. We seldom realize, for example, that our most
private thoughts and emotions are not actually our own.
For we think in terms of languages and images which
we did not invent, but which were given to us by our
society. We copy emotional reactions from our parents,
learning from them that excrement is supposed to have
a disgusting smell and that vomiting is supposed to be
an unpleasant sensation. The dread of death is also
learned from their anxieties about sickness and from
their attitudes to funerals and corpses. Our social environment has this power just because we do not exist
apart from a society. Society is our extended mind and
body.

Yet the very society from which the individual is
inseparable is using its whole irresistible force to persuade the individual that he is indeed separate! Society
as we now know it is therefore playing a game
with self-contradictory rules. Just because we do not
exist apart from the community, the community is
able to convince us that we do—that each one of us is

an independent source of action with a mind of its own. The more successfully the community implants this feeling, the more trouble it has in getting the individual to cooperate, with the result that children raised in such an environment are almost permanently confused.

This state of affairs is known technically as the "double-bind." A person is put in a double-bind by a command or request which contains a concealed contradiction. "Stop being self-conscious!" "Try to relax." Or the famous prosecuting attorney's question to the man accused of cruelty to his wife—"Have you stopped beating your wife yet? Answer yes or no." This is a damned-if-you-do and damned-if-you-don't situation which arises constantly in human (and especially family) relations. A wife complains to her husband, "Do you realize that since we were married two years ago you haven't once taken me to the movies? It wasn't that way when you were courting. I think you're beginning to take me for granted." When the penitent husband returns from work the following evening he says, "Darling, what about going to the movies after dinner?" And she replies, "You're only suggesting it because I complained!"

Society, as we now have it, pulled this trick on every child from earliest infancy. In the first place, the child is taught that he is responsible, that he is a free agent, an independent origin of thoughts and actions—a sort of miniature First Cause. He accepts this make-believe for the very reason that it is not true. He can't help accepting it, just as he can't help accepting membership in the community where he was born. He has no way of resisting this kind of social indoctrination. It is constantly reinforced with rewards and punishments. It is built into the basic structure of the language he is learning. It is rubbed in repeatedly with such remarks as, "It isn't like you to do a thing like that." Or, "Don't be a copy-cat; be yourself!" Or, when one child imitates the mannerisms of another child whom he admires, "Johnny, that's not you. That's Peter!" the innocent victim of this indoctrination cannot understand the paradox. He is being told that he *must* be free. An irresistible pressure is being put on him to make him believe that no such pressure exists. The community of which he is necessarily a dependent member defines him as an independent member.

In the second place, he is thereupon commanded, as a free agent, to do things which will be acceptable only if done voluntarily! "You really *ought* to love us," say parents, aunts, uncles, brothers, and sisters. "All nice children love their families, and do things for them without having to be asked." In other words, "We demand that you love us because you want to, and not because we say you ought to." Part of this nonsense is due to the fact that we confuse the "must" expressing a condition ("To be human you must have a head") with the "must" expressing a command ("You must put away your toys"). No one makes an effort to have a head, and yet parents insist that, to be healthy, a child "must" have regular bowel movements, or that he must *try* to go to sleep, or that he must make an effort to pay attention—as if these goals were simply to be achieved by muscular exertion.

Children are in no position to see the contradictions in these demands, and even if some prodigy were to point them out, he would be told summarily not to "answer back," and that he lacked respect for his "elders and betters." Instead of giving our children clear and explicit explanations of the game-rules of the community, we befuddle them hopelessly because we—as adults—were once so befuddled, and, remaining so, do not understand the game we are playing.

A double-bind game is a game with self-contradictory rules, a game doomed to perpetual self-frustration—like trying to invent a perpetual-motion machine in terms of Newtonian mechanics, or trying to trisect any given angle with a straightedge and compass. The social double-bind game can be phrased in several ways:

> The first rule of this game is that it is not a game.
> Everyone must play.
> You must love us.
> You must go on living.
> Be yourself, but play a consistent and acceptable role.
> Control yourself and be natural.
> Try to be sincere.

Essentially, this game is a demand for spontaneous behavior of certain kinds. Living, loving, being natural or sincere—all these are spontaneous forms of behavior: they happen "of themselves" like digesting food or growing hair. As soon as they are forced they acquire that unnatural, contrived, and phony atmosphere which everyone deplores—weak and scentless like forced flowers and tasteless like forced fruit. Life and love generate effort, but effort will not generate them. Faith—in life, in other people, and in oneself—is the attitude of allowing the spontaneous to *be* spontaneous, in its own way and in its own time. This is, of course, risky because life and other people do not always respond to faith as we might wish. Faith is always a gamble because life itself is a gambling game with what must appear, in the hiding aspect of the game, to be colossal stakes. But to take the gamble out of the game, to try to make winning a dead certainty, is to achieve a certainty which is indeed dead. The alternative to a community based on mutual trust is a totalitarian police-state, a community in which spontaneity is virtually forbidden.

A Hindu treatise on the art of government, the *Arthashastra,* lays down the rules of policy for the complete tyrant, describing the organization of his palace, his court, and his state in such fashion as to make Machiavelli seem a liberal. The first rule is that he must trust no one, and be without a single intimate friend. Beyond this, he must organize his government as a series of concentric circles composed of the various ministers, generals, officers, secretaries, and servants who execute his orders, every circle constituting a degree of rank leading up to the king himself at the center—like a spider in its web. Beginning with the circle immediately surrounding the king, the circles must consist alternately of his natural enemies and his natural friends. Because the very highest rank of princes will be plotting to seize the king's power, they must be surrounded and watched by a circle of ministers eager to gain the king's favor—and this hierarchy of mutually mistrusting circles must go all the way out to the fringe of the web. *Divide et impera*—divide and rule.

Meanwhile, the king remains in the safety of his inmost apartments, attended by guards who are in turn watched by other guards hidden in the walls. Slaves taste his food for poison, and he must sleep either with one eye open or with his door firmly locked on the inside. In case of a serious revolution, there must be a secret, underground passage giving him escape from the center—a passage containing a lever which will unsettle the keystone of the building and bring it crashing down upon his rebellious court. The *Arthashastra* does not forget to warn the tyrant that he can never win. He may rise to eminence through ambition or the call of duty, but the more absolute his power, the more he is hated, and the more he is the prisoner of his own trap. The web catches the spider. He cannot wander at leisure in the streets and parks of his own capital, or sit on a lonely beach listening to the waves and watching the gulls. Through enslaving others he himself becomes the most miserable of slaves.

Nothing fails like success—because the self-imposed task of our society and all its members is a contradiction: to force things to happen which are acceptable only when they happen without force. This, in turn, arises from the definition of man as an independent agent—*in* the universe but not *of* it—saddled with the job of bending the world to his will. No amount of preaching and moralizing will tame the type of man so defined, for the hypnotic hallucination of himself as something separate from the world renders him incapable of seeing that life is a system of geological and biological cooperation. Certainly, the system *contains* fights: birds against worms, snails against lettuce, and spiders against flies. But these fights are contained in the sense that they do not get out of hand, that no one species is the permanent victor. Man alone is trying to *eliminate* his natural enemies in the conviction that he is, or should be, the supreme species. Just as we cultivate vegetables, cattle, and chickens for food in the realization that we depend upon these creatures for our life, we should also realize that enemy creatures which prey upon man—insects, bacteria, and various fungi—are in fact enemy/friends.

A New York hostess entertaining a statesman from Pakistan brought up the problem of the urgent need for birth-control in Asia, and what was being done about it in Pakistan. She was utterly nonplussed with the reply that all the propaganda about birth-control was merely the white man's attempt to maintain his superiority over the colored races. I told her that she should have answered, "No, indeed. We only want to help you to prune your beautiful fruit-trees."

For the enemy/friends of man are his pruners. They prevent him from destroying himself by excess fertility, so that a person who dies of malaria or tuberculosis should be honored at least as much as one who has died for his country in battle. He has made room for the rest of us, and the bacteria which killed him should be saluted with proper chivalry as an honorable foe. The point is not that we should forthwith abandon penicillin or DDT: it is that we should fight to check the enemy, not to eliminate him. We must learn to include ourselves in the round of cooperations and conflicts, of symbiosis and preying, which constitutes the balance of nature, for a permanently victorious species destroys, not only itself, but all other life in its environment.

The obvious objection to an argument against "wiping out" such natural enemies of man as cancer or mosquitoes is our sympathy for the individuals who get caught. It is all very well to reason, in the abstract, that the human population has to be pruned, but when disease puts its finger on me I run for the doctor. What would be the success of a call for "volunteers for pruning"? In Western civilization we do not abandon sickly babies, shoot the insane, let the hungry starve, or leave diseased people to die on the streets. (At least, not in our better moments.) For the most sacred ideal of our culture is the right of every individual to justice, health, and wealth, or "life, liberty, and the pursuit of happiness." To suggest that the personal ego is a hallucination seems to be an attack on this most sacred value, without which civilized people would fall back to the level of coolies or ants to become an organized mass where the particular person is expendable.

During World War II a friend of mine used to fly Chinese laborers over the Hump to work on the South end of the Burma Road. The long flight was, of course, ideal for gambling, but since there was not enough cash between them to make the game interesting, the stakes were that the final loser should jump off the plane. No parachute. Our natural reaction is that such people aren't fully human. Like the families and servants of ancient kings who were buried alive with their deceased lord, they seem, as Thomas Mann suggested, to be faces with no back to their heads—mere masks, mere roles of no further use or meaning; bees without a queen. Whatever villainies the British may have committed in India, their Christian consciences balked at the practice of *sati,* which required a widow to commit suicide at her husband's funeral. Truly civilized people are—we feel—not faces on the sky but fully enclosed heads containing souls, each one of infinite value in the sight of God.

At one extreme, then, we have the sacred individual—the unique personal ego, separate from both nature and God—defined as such by a society which, almost in the same breath, commands him to be free and commands him to conform. At the other extreme is the coolie, the cog in the industrial-collectivist machine, or the mere "hand" (as the factory worker is often called). If one believes that the personal ego is a natural endowment of all men, as distinct from a social convention, then the lot of the coolie is bleak indeed—for one sees him as a repressed and frustrated person, though his own society may never have defined him as such.

However, there is a third possibility. The individual may be understood neither as an isolated person nor as an expendable, humanoid working-machine. He may be seen, instead, as one particular focal point at which the whole universe expresses itself—as an incarnation of the Self, of the Godhead, or whatever one may choose to call IT. This view retains and, indeed, amplifies our apprehension that the individual is in some way sacred. At the same time it dissolves the paradox of the personal ego, which is to have attained the "precious state" of being a unique person at the price of perpetual anxiety for one's survival. The hallucination of separateness prevents one from seeing that to cherish the ego is to cherish misery. We do not realize that our so-called love and concern for the individual is simply the other face of our own fear of death or rejection. In his exaggerated valuation of separate identity, the personal ego is sawing off the branch on which he is sitting, and then getting more and more anxious about the coming crash!

Let it be clear, furthermore, that the ego-fiction is in no way essential to the individual, to the total human organism, in fulfilling and expressing his individuality. For every individual is a unique manifestation of the Whole, as every branch is a particular outreaching of the tree. To manifest individuality, every branch must have a sensitive connection with the tree, just as our independently moving and differentiated fingers must have a sensitive connection with the whole body. The point, which can hardly be repeated too often, is that differentiation is not separation. The head and the feet are different, but not separate, and though man is not connected to the universe by exactly the same physical relation as branch to tree or feet to head, he is none-theless connected—and by physical relations of fascinating complexity. The death of the individual is not disconnection but simply withdrawal. The corpse is like a footprint or an echo—the dissolving trace of something which the Self has ceased to do.

If, then, the differentiation of individuals is of great value, on the principle that variety is the spice of life, this value is not going to be enhanced by a self-contradictory definition of individuality. Our society—that is, we ourselves, all of us—is defining the individual with a double-bind, commanding him to be free and separate from the world, which he is not, for otherwise the command would not work. Under the circumstances, it works only in the sense of implanting an illusion of separateness, just as the commands of a hypnotist can create illusions.

Thus bamboozled, the individual—instead of fulfilling his unique function in the world—is exhausted and frustrated in efforts to accomplish self-contradictory goals. Because he is now so largely defined as a separate person caught up in a mindless and alien universe, his principal task is to get one-up on the universe and to conquer nature. This is palpably absurd, and since the task is never achieved, the individual is taught to live and work for some future in which the impossible will at last happen, if not for him, then at least for his children. We are thus breeding a type of human being incapable of living in the present—that is, of really living.

For unless one is able to live fully in the present, the future is a hoax. There is no point whatever in making plans for a future which you will never be able to enjoy. When your plans mature, you will still be living for some other future beyond. You will never, never be able to sit back with full contentment and say, "Now, I've arrived!" Your entire education has deprived you of this capacity because it was preparing you for the future, instead of showing you how to be alive now.

In other words, you have been hypnotized or conditioned by an educational processing-system arranged in grades or steps, supposedly leading to some ultimate Success. First nursery school or kindergarten, then the grades or forms of elementary school, preparing you for the great moment of secondary school! But then more steps, up and up to the coveted goal of the university. Here, if you are clever, you can stay on indefinitely by getting into graduate school and becoming a permanent student. Otherwise, you are headed step by step for the great Outside World of family-raising, business, and profession. Yet graduation day is a very temporary fulfillment, for with your first sales-promotion meeting you are back in the same old system, being urged to make that quota (and if you do, they'll give you a higher quota) and so progress up the ladder to sales manager, vice-president, and, at last, president of your own show (about forty to forty-five years old). In the meantime, the insurance and investment people have been interesting you in plans for Retirement—that really ultimate goal of being able to sit back and enjoy the fruits of all your labors. But when that day comes, your anxieties and exertions will have left you with a weak heart, false teeth, prostate trouble, sexual impotence, fuzzy eyesight, and a vile digestion.

All this might have been wonderful if, at every stage, you had been able to play it as a game, finding your work as fascinating as poker, chess, or fishing. But for most of us the day is divided into work-time and play-time, the work consisting largely of tasks which others pay us to do because they are abysmally uninteresting. We therefore work, not for the work's sake, but for money—and money is supposed to get us what we really want in our hours of leisure and play. In the United States even poor people have lots of money compared with the wretched and skinny millions of India, Africa, and China, while our middle and upper classes (or should we say "income groups"?) are as prosperous as princes. Yet, by and large, they have but slight taste for pleasure. Money alone cannot buy pleasure, though it can help. For enjoyment is an art and a skill for which we have little talent or energy.

I live close to a harbor packed with sailing-boats and luxurious cruisers which are seldom used, because seamanship is a difficult though rewarding art which their owners have no time to practice. They bought the boats either as status symbols or as toys, but on discovering that they were not toys (as advertised) they lost interest. The same is true of the entire and astounding abundance of pleasure-goods that we can buy. Foodstuffs are prolific, but few know how to cook. Building materials abound in both quantity and variety, yet most homes look as if they had been made by someone who had heard of a house but never seen one. Silks, linens, wools, and cottons are available in colors and patterns galore, and yet most men dress like divinity students or undertakers, while women are slaves to the fashion game with its basic rule, "I have conformed sooner than you." The market for artists and sculptors has thrived as never before in history, but the paintings look as if they had been made with excrement or scraps from billboards, and the sculptures like mangled typewriters or charred lumber from a burned-down outhouse.[2] We have untold stacks of recorded music from every age and culture, and the most superb means of playing it. But who actually listens? Maybe a few pot-smokers.

[2]This is not to be taken as a rejection of "modern art" in general, but only of that rather dominant aspect of it which claims that the artist should represent his time. And since this is the time of junkyards, billboards, and expensive slums, many artists—otherwise bereft of talent—make a name for themselves by the "tasteful" framing or pedestaling of objets trouvés from the city dump.

This is perhaps a Henry Millerish exaggeration. Nevertheless, it strikes me more and more that America's reputation for materialism is unfounded—that is, if a materialist is a person who thoroughly enjoys the physical world and loves material things. In this sense, we are superb materialists when it comes to the construction of jet aircraft, but when we decorate the inside of these magnificent monsters for the comfort of passengers it is nothing but frippery. High-heeled, narrow-hipped, doll-type girls serving imitation, warmed-over meals. For our pleasures are not material pleasures but *symbols* of pleasure—attractively packaged but inferior in content.

The explanation is simple: most of our products are being made by people who do not enjoy making them, whether as owners or workers. Their aim in the enterprise is not the product but money, and therefore every trick is used to cut the cost of production and hoodwink the buyer, by coloring and packaging chicanery, into the belief that the product is well and truly made. The only exceptions are those products which simply *must* be excellent for reasons of safety or high cost of purchase—aircraft, computers, space-rockets, scientific instruments, and so forth.

But the whole scheme is a vicious circle, for when you have made the money what will you buy with it? Other pretentious fakes made by other money-mad manufacturers. The few real luxuries on the market are imports from "backward" countries where peasants and craftsmen still take pride in their work. For example, the state of Oaxaca in Mexico produces some of the finest blankets in the world, and American buyers have been trying to import them in huge quantities. But no amount of money will give the relatively few craftsmen who weave them time to fill the order. If they want the order, they must begin to cheat and produce inferior blankets. The only solution would be to train hundreds of new craftsmen. But Oaxaca is just getting television and has, for some time, had public education, so what up-and-coming young person would want to waste his days weaving blankets?

The poets and sages have, indeed, been saying for centuries that success in this world is vanity. "The worldly hope men set their hearts upon turns ashes," or, as we might put it in a more up-to-date idiom, just when our mouth was watering for the ultimate goodies, it turns out to be a mixture of plaster-of-paris, papier-mâché, and plastic glue. Comes in any flavor. I have thought of putting this on the market as a universal substance, a *prima materia,* for making anything and everything—houses, furniture, flowers, bread (they use it already), apples, and even people.

The world, they are saying, is a mirage. Everything is forever falling apart and there's no way of fixing it, and the more strenuously you grasp this airy nothingness, the more swiftly it collapses in your hands. Western, technological civilization is, thus far, man's most desperate effort to beat the game—to understand, control, and fix this will-o'-the-wisp called life, and it may be that its very strength and skill will all the more rapidly dissolve its dreams. But if this is not to be so, technical power must be in the hands of a new kind of man.

In times past, recognition of the impermanence of the world usually led to withdrawal. On the one hand, ascetics, monks, and hermits tried to exorcise their desires so as to regard the world with benign resignation, or to draw back and back into the depths of consciousness to become one with the Self in its unmanifest state of eternal serenity. On the other hand, others felt that the world was a state of probation where material goods were to be used in a spirit of stewardship, as loans from the Almighty, and where the main work of life is loving devotion to God and to man.

Yet both these responses are based on the initial supposition that the individual is the separate ego, and because this supposition is the work of a double-bind any task undertaken on this basis—including religion—will be self-defeating. Just because it is a hoax from the beginning, the personal ego can make only a phony response to life. For the world is an ever-elusive and ever-disappointing mirage only from the standpoint of someone standing aside from it—as if it were quite other than himself—and then trying to grasp it. Without birth and death, and without the perpetual transmutation of all the forms of life, the world would be static, rhythmless, undancing, mummified.

But a third response is possible. Not withdrawal, not stewardship on the hypothesis of a *future* reward, but the fullest collaboration with the world as a harmonious system of contained conflicts—based on the realization that the only real "I" is the whole endless process. This realization is already in us in the sense that our bodies know it, our bones and nerves and sense-organs. We do not know it only in the sense that the thin ray of conscious attention has been taught to ignore it, and taught so thoroughly that we are very genuine fakes indeed.

Four

THE WORLD IS YOUR BODY

We have now found out that many things which we felt to be basic realities of nature are social fictions, arising from commonly accepted or traditional ways of thinking about the world. These fictions have included:

1. The notion that the world is made up or composed of separate bits or things.

2. That things are differing forms of some basic stuff.

3. That individual organisms are such things, and that they are inhabited and partially controlled by independent egos.

4. That the opposite poles of relationships, such as light/darkness and solid/space, are in actual conflict which may result in the permanent victory of one of the poles.

5. That death is evil, and that life must be a constant war against it.

6. That man, individually and collectively, should aspire to be top species and put himself in control of nature.

Fictions are useful so long as they are taken as fictions. They are then simply ways of "figuring" the world which we agree to follow so that we can act in cooperation, as we agree about inches and hours, numbers and words, mathematical systems and languages. If we have no agreement about measures of time and space, I would have no way of making a date with you at the corner of Forty-second Street and Fifth Avenue at 3 P.M. on Sunday, April 4.

But the troubles begin when the fictions are taken as facts. Thus in 1752 the British government instituted a calendar reform which required that September 2 of that year be dated September 14, with the result that many people imagined that eleven days had been taken off their lives, and rushed to Westminster screaming, "Give us back our eleven days!" Such confusions of fact and fiction make it all the more difficult to find wider acceptance of common laws, languages, measures, and other useful institutions, and to improve those already employed.

But, as we have seen, the deeper troubles arise when we confuse ourselves and our fundamental relationships to the world with fictions (or figures of thought) which are taken for granted, unexamined, and often self-contradictory. Here, as we have also seen, the "nub" problem is the self-contradictory definition of man himself as a separate and independent being *in* the world, as distinct from a special action *of* the world. Part of our difficulty is that the latter view of man seems to make him no more than a puppet, but this is because, in trying to accept or understand the latter view, we are still in the grip of the former. To say that man is an action of the world is *not* to define him as a "thing" which is helplessly pushed around by all other "things." We have to get beyond Newton's vision of the world as a system of billiard balls in which every individual ball is passively knocked about by all the rest! Remember that Aristotle's and Newton's preoccupation with causal determinism was that they were trying to explain how one thing or event was influenced by others, forgetting that the division of the world into separate things and events was a fiction. To say that certain events are causally connected is only a clumsy way of saying that they are features of the same event, like the head and tail of the cat.

It is essential to understand this point thoroughly: that the thing-in-itself (Kant's *ding an sich*), whether animal, vegetable, or mineral, is not only unknowable— it does not exist. This is important not only for sanity and peace of mind, but also for the most "practical" reasons of economics, politics, and technology. Our practical projects have run into confusion again and again through failure to see that individual people, nations, animals, insects, and plants do not exist in or by themselves. This is not to say only that things exist in relation to one another, but that what we call "things" are no more than glimpses of a unified process. Certainly, this process has distinct features which catch our attention, but we must remember that distinction is not separation. Sharp and clear as the crest of the wave may be, it necessarily "goes with" the smooth and less featured curve of the trough. So also the bright points of the stars "gowith" (if I may now coin a word) the dark background of space.

In the Gestalt theory of perception this is known as the figure/ground relationship. This theory asserts, in brief, that no figure is ever perceived except in relation to a background. If, for example, you come so close to me that the outline of my body lies beyond your field of vision, the "thing" you will see will no longer be my body. Your attention will instead be "captured" by a coat-button or a necktie, for the theory also asserts that, against any given background, our attention is almost automatically "won" by any moving shape (in contrast with the stationary background) or by any enclosed or tightly complex feature (in contrast with the simpler, featureless background).

Thus when I draw the following figure on a blackboard—

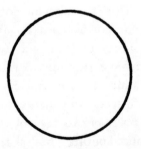

and ask, "What have I drawn?" people will generally identify it as a circle, a ball, a disk, or a ring. Only rarely will someone reply, "A wall with a hole in it."

In other words, we do not easily notice that all features of the world hold their boundaries in common
with the areas that surround them—that the outline of
the figure is also the inline of the background. Let us
suppose that my circle/hole figure were to move
through the following series of shapes:

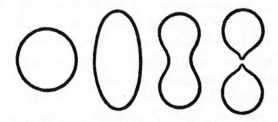

Most people would thereupon ascribe the movement,
the act, to the enclosed area as if it were an amoeba.
But I might just as well have been drawing the dry
patches in a thin film of water spread over a polished
table. But the point is that, in either case, the movement
of any feature of the world cannot be ascribed to the
outside alone or to the inside alone. Both move together.

Our difficulty in noticing both the presence and the
action of the background in these simple illustrations is
immensely increased when it comes to the behavior of
living organisms. When we watch ants scurrying hither
and thither over a patch of sand, or people milling
around in a public square, it seems absolutely undeniable that the ants and the people are alone responsible
for the movement. Yet in fact this is only a highly
complex version of the simple problem of the three balls
moving in space, in which we had to settle for the so-

lution that the entire configuration (Gestalt) is moving—not the balls alone, not the space alone, not even the balls and the space together in concert, but rather a single field of solid/space of which the balls and the space are, as it were, poles.

The illusion that organisms move entirely on their own is immensely persuasive until we settle down, as scientists do, to describe their behavior carefully. Then the scientist, be he biologist, sociologist, or physicist, finds very rapidly that he cannot say what the organism is doing unless, at the same time, he describes the behavior of its surroundings. Obviously, an organism cannot be described as walking just in terms of leg motion, for the direction and speed of this walking must be described in terms of the ground upon which it moves. Furthermore, this walking is seldom haphazard. It has something to do with food-sources in the area, with the hostile or friendly behavior of other organisms, and countless other factors which we do not immediately consider when attention is first drawn to a prowling ant. The more detailed the description of our ant's behavior becomes, the more it has to include such matters as density, humidity, and temperature of the surrounding atmosphere, the types and sources of its food, the social structure of its own species, and that of neighboring species with which it has some symbiotic or preying relationship.

When at last the whole vast list is compiled, and the scientist calls "Finish!" for lack of further time or interest, he may well have the impression that the ant's behavior is no more than its automatic and involuntary reaction to its environment. It is attracted by this, repelled by that, kept alive by one condition, and destroyed by another. But let us suppose that he turns his attention to some other organism in the ant's neighborhood—perhaps a housewife with a greasy kitchen— he will soon have to include that ant, and all its friends and relations, as something which determines *her* behavior! Wherever he turns his attention, he finds, instead of some positive, causal agent, a merely responsive hollow whose boundaries go this way and that according to outside pressures.

Yet, on second thought, this won't do. What does it *mean,* he asks himself, that a description of what the ant is doing must include what its environment is doing? It means that the thing or entity he is studying and describing has changed. It started out to be the individual ant, but it very quickly became the whole field of activities in which the ant is found. The same thing would happen if one started out to describe a particular organ of the body: it would be utterly unintelligible unless one took into account its relationships with other organs. It is thus that every scientific discipline for the study of living organisms—bacteriology, botany, zoology, biology, anthropology—must, from its own special standpoint, develop a science of ecology—literally, "the logic of the household"—or the study of organism/environment fields. Unfortunately, this science runs afoul of academic politics, being much too interdisciplinary for the jealous guardians of departmental boundaries. But the neglect of ecology is the one most serious weakness of modern technology, and it goes hand-in-hand with our reluctance to be participating members of the whole community of living species.

Man aspires to *govern* nature, but the more one studies ecology, the more absurd it seems to speak of any one feature of an organism, or of an organism/environment field, as governing or ruling others. Once upon a time the mouth, the hands, and the feet said to each other, "We do all this work gathering food and chewing it up, but the lazy fellow, the stomach, does nothing. It's high time he did some work too, so let's go on strike!" Whereupon they went many days without working, but soon found themselves feeling weaker and weaker until at last each of them realized that the stomach was *their* stomach, and that they would have to go back to work to remain alive. But even in physiological textbooks, we speak of the brain, or the nervous system, as "governing" the heart or the digestive tract, smuggling bad politics into science, as if the heart belonged to the brain rather than the brain to the heart or the stomach. Yet it is as true, or false, to say that the brain "feeds itself" through the stomach as that the stomach "evolves" a brain at its upper entrance to get more food.

As soon as one sees that separate things are fictitious, it becomes obvious that nonexistent things cannot "perform" actions. The difficulty is that most languages are arranged so that actions (verbs) have to be set in motion by things (nouns), and we forget that rules of grammar are not necessarily rules, or patterns, of nature. This, which is nothing more than a convention of grammar, is also responsible for (or, better, "goes-with") absurd puzzles as to how spirit governs matter, or mind moves body. How can a noun, which is by definition *not* action, lead to action?

Scientists would be less embarrassed if they used a

language, on the model of Amerindian Nootka, consisting of verbs and adverbs, and leaving off nouns and adjectives. If we can speak of a house as housing, a mat as matting, or of a couch as seating, why can't we think of people as "peopling," of brains as "braining," or of an ant as an "anting?" Thus in the Nootka language a church is "housing religiously," a shop is "housing tradingly," and a home is "housing homely." Yet we are habituated to ask, "Who or what is housing? Who peoples? What is it that ants?" Yet isn't it obvious that when we say, "The lightning flashed," the flashing is the same as the lightning, and that it would be enough to say, "There was lightning"? Everything labeled with a noun is demonstrably a process or action, but language is full of spooks, like the "it" in "It is raining," which are the supposed causes of action.

Does it really explain running to say that "A man is running"? On the contrary, the only explanation would be a description of the field or situation in which "a manning goeswith running" as distinct from one in which "a manning goeswith sitting." (I am not recommending this primitive and clumsy form of verb language for general and normal use. We should have to contrive something much more elegant.) Furthermore, running is not something other than myself, which I (the organism) *do*. For the organism is sometimes a running process, sometimes a standing process, sometimes a sleeping process, and so on, and in each instance the "cause" of the behavior is the situation as a whole, the organism/environment. Indeed, it would be best to drop the idea of causality and use instead the idea of relativity.

For it is still inexact to say that an organism "responds" or "reacts" to a given situation by running or standing, or whatever. This is still the language of Newtonian billiards. It is easier to think of situations as moving patterns, like organisms themselves. Thus, to go back to the cat (or catting), a situation with pointed ears and whiskers at one end does not have a tail at the other as a response or reaction to the whiskers, or the claws, or the fur. As the Chinese say, the various features of a situation "arise mutually" or imply one another as back implies front, and as chickens imply eggs—and vice versa. They exist in relation to each other like the poles of the magnet, only more complexly patterned.

Moreover, as the egg/chicken relation suggests, not all the features of a total situation have to appear at the same time. The existence of a man implies parents, even though they may be long since dead, and the birth of an organism implies its death. Wouldn't it be as far-fetched to call birth the cause of death as to call the cat's head the cause of the tail? Lifting the neck of a bottle implies lifting the bottom as well, for the "two parts" come up at the same time. If I pick up an accordion by one end, the other will follow a little later, but the principle is the same. Total situations are, therefore, patterns in time as much as patterns in space.

And, right now is the moment to say that I am not trying to smuggle in the "total situation" as a new disguise for the old "things" which were supposed to explain behavior or action. The total situation or field is always open-ended, for

> *Little fields have big fields*
> *Upon their backs to bite 'em,*

*And big fields have bigger fields
And so* ad infinitum.

We can never, never describe *all* features of the total situation, not only because every situation is infinitely complex, but also because the *total* situation is the universe. Fortunately, we do not have to describe any situation exhaustively, because some of its features appear to be much more important than others for understanding the behavior of the various organisms within it. We never get more than a sketch of the situation, yet this is enough to show that actions (or processes) must be understood, or explained, in terms of situations just as words must be understood in the context of sentences, paragraphs, chapters, books, libraries, and . . . life itself.

To sum up: just as no thing or organism exists on its own, it does not act on its own. Furthermore, every organism is a process: thus the organism is not other than its actions. To put it clumsily: it is what it does. More precisely, the organism, including its behavior, is a process which is to be understood only in relation to the larger and longer process of its environment. For what we mean by "understanding" or "comprehension" is seeing how parts fit into a whole, and then realizing that they don't *compose* the whole, as one assembles a jigsaw puzzle, but that the whole is a pattern, a complex wiggliness, which *has* no separate parts. Parts are fictions of language, of the calculus of looking at the world through a net which *seems* to chop it up into bits. Parts exist only for purposes of figuring and describing, and as we figure the world out we become confused if we do not remember this all the time.

Once this is clear, we have shattered the myth of the Fully Automatic Universe where human consciousness and intelligence are a fluke in the midst of boundless stupidity. For if the behavior of an organism is intelligible only in relation to its environment, intelligent behavior implies an intelligent environment. Obviously, if "parts" do not really exist, it makes no sense to speak of an intelligent part of an unintelligent whole. It is easy enough to see that an intelligent human being implies an intelligent human society, for thinking is a social activity—a mutual interchange of messages and ideas based on such social institutions as languages, sciences, libraries, universities, and museums. But what about the non-human environment in which human society flourishes?

Ecologists often speak of the "evolution of environments" over and above the evolution of organisms. For man did not appear on earth until the earth itself, together with all its biological forms, had evolved to a certain degree of balance and complexity. At this point of evolution the earth "implied" man, just as the existence of man implies that sort of a planet at that stage of evolution. The balance of nature, the "harmony of contained conflicts," in which man thrives is a network of mutually interdependent organisms of the most astounding subtlety and complexity. Teilhard de Chardin has called it the "biosphere," the film of living organisms which covers the original "geosphere," the mineral planet. Lack of knowledge about the evolution of the organic from the "inorganic," coupled with misleading myths about life coming "into" this world from somewhere "outside," has made it difficult for us to see that the biosphere arises, or goeswith, a certain degree of geological and astronomical evolution. But, as Douglas E. Harding has pointed out, we tend to think of this planet as a life-infested rock, which is as absurd as thinking of the human body as a cell-infested skeleton. Surely all forms of life, including man, must be understood as "symptoms" of the earth, the solar system, and the galaxy—in which case we cannot escape the conclusion that the galaxy is intelligent.

If I first see a tree in the winter, I might assume that it is not a fruit-tree. But when I return in the summer to find it covered with plums, I must exclaim, "Excuse me! You were a fruit-tree after all." Imagine, then, that a billion years ago some beings from another part of the galaxy made a tour through the solar system in their flying saucer and found no life. They would dismiss it as "Just a bunch of old rocks!" But if they returned today, they would have to apologize: "Well—you were peopling rocks after all!" You may, of course, argue that there is no analogy between the two situations. The fruit-tree was at one time a seed inside a plum, but the earth—much less the solar system or the galaxy—was never a seed inside a person. But, oddly enough, you would be wrong.

I have tried to explain that the relation between an organism and its environment is *mutual,* that neither one is the "cause" or determinant of the other since the arrangement between them is polar. If, then, it makes sense to explain the organism and its behavior in terms of the environment, it will also make sense to explain the environment in terms of the organism. (Thus far I have kept this up my sleeve so as not to confuse the first aspect of the picture.) For there is a very real, physical sense in which man, and every other organism, creates his own environment.

Our whole knowledge of the world is, in one sense, self-knowledge. For knowing is a translation of external events into bodily processes, and especially into states of the nervous system and the brain: we know the world *in terms* of the body, and in accordance with its structure. Surgical alterations of the nervous system, or, in all probability, sense-organs of a different structure than ours, give different types of perception—just as the microscope and telescope change the vision of the naked eye. Bees and other insects have, for example, polaroid eyes which enable them to tell the position of the sun by observing any patch of blue sky. In other words, because of the different structure of their eyes, the sky that they see is not the sky that we see. Bats and homing pigeons have sensory equipment analogous to radar, and in this respect see more "reality" than we do without our special instruments.

From the viewpoint of your eyes your own head seems to be an invisible blank, neither dark nor light, standing immediately behind the nearest thing you can see. But in fact the whole field of vision "out there in front" is a sensation in the lower back of your head, where the optical centers of the brain are located. What you see out there is, immediately, how the inside of your head "looks" or "feels." So, too, everything that you hear, touch, taste, and smell is some kind of vibration interacting with your brain, which translates that vibration into what you know as light, color, sound, hardness, roughness, saltiness, heaviness, or pungence. Apart from your brain, all these vibrations would be like the sound of one hand clapping, or of sticks playing on a skinless drum. Apart from your brain, or some brain, the world is devoid of light, heat, weight, solidity, motion, space, time, or any other imaginable feature. All these phenomena are interactions, or transactions, of vibrations with a certain arrangement of neurons. Thus vibrations of light and heat from the sun do not actually become light or heat until they interact with a living organism, just as no light-beams are visible in space unless reflected by particles of atmosphere or dust. In other words, it "takes two" to make anything happen. As we saw, a single ball in space has no motion, whereas two balls give the possibility of linear motion, three balls motion in a plane, and four balls motion in three dimensions.

The same is true for the activation of an electric current. No current will "flow" through a wire until the positive pole is connected with the negative, or, to put it very simply, no current will start unless it has a point of arrival, and a living organism is a "point of arrival" apart from which there can never be the "currents" or phenomena of light, heat, weight, hardness, and so forth. One might almost say that the magic of the brain is to evoke these marvels from the universe, as a harpist evokes melody from the silent strings.

A still more cogent example of existence as relationship is the production of a rainbow.[1] For a rainbow appears only when there is a certain triangular relationship between three components: the sun, moisture in

[1] For this illustration I am indebted to Owen Barfield, *Saving the Appearances*. Faber & Faber, London, 1956.

the atmosphere, and an observer. If all three are present, and if the angular relationship between them is correct, then, and then only, will there be the phenomenon "rainbow." Diaphanous as it may be, a rainbow is no subjective hallucination. It can be verified by any number of observers, though each will see it in a slightly different position. As a boy, I once chased the end of a rainbow on my bicycle and was amazed to find that it always receded. It was like trying to catch the reflection of the moon on water. I did not then understand that no rainbow would appear unless the sun, and I, and the invisible center of the bow were on the same straight line, so that I changed the apparent position of the bow as I moved.

The point is, then, that an observer in the proper position is as necessary for the manifestation of a rainbow as the other two components, the sun and the moisture. Of course, one could say that if the sun and a body of moisture were in the right relationship, say, over the ocean, any observer on a ship that sailed into line with them would see a rainbow. But one could also say that if an observer and the sun were correctly aligned there would be a rainbow if there were moisture in the air!

Somehow the first set of conditions seems to preserve the reality of the rainbow apart from an observer. But the second set, by eliminating a good, solid "external reality," seems to make it an indisputable fact that, under such conditions, there is no rainbow. The reason is only that it supports our current mythology to assert that things exist on their own, whether there is an observer or not. It supports the fantasy that man is not really involved in the world, that he makes no real difference to it, and that he can observe reality independently without changing it. For the myth of this solid and sensible physical world which is "there," whether we see it or not, goes hand-in-hand with the myth that every observer is a separate ego, "confronted" with a reality quite other than himself.

Perhaps we can accept this reasoning without too much struggle when it concerns things like rainbows and reflections, whose reality status was never too high. But what if it dawns on us that our perception of rocks, mountains, and stars is a situation of just the same kind? There is nothing in the least unreasonable about this. We have not had to drag in any such spooks as mind, soul, or spirit. We have simply been talking of an interaction between physical vibrations and the brain with its various organs of sense, saying only that creatures with brains are an *integral* feature of the pattern which also includes the solid earth and the stars, and that without this integral feature (or pole of the current) the whole cosmos would be as unmanifested as a rainbow without droplets in the sky, or without an observer. Our resistance to this reasoning is psychological. It makes us feel insecure because it unsettles a familiar image of the world in which rocks, above all, are symbols of hard, unshakable reality, and the Eternal Rock a metaphor for God himself. The mythology of the nineteenth century had reduced man to an utterly unimportant little germ in an unimaginably vast and enduring universe. It is just too much of a shock, too fast a switch, to recognize that this little germ with its fabulous brain is evoking the whole thing, including the nebulae millions of light-years away.

Does this force us to the highly implausible conclusion that before the first living organism came into being equipped with a brain there *was* no universe—that the organic and inorganic phenomena came into existence at the same temporal moment? Is it possible that all geological and astronomical history is a mere extrapolation—that it is talking about what *would* have happened *if* it had been observed? Perhaps. But I will venture a more cautious idea. The fact that every organism evokes its own environment must be corrected with the polar or opposite fact that the total environment evokes the organism. Furthermore, the total environment (or situation) is both spatial and temporal—both larger and longer than the organisms contained in its field. The organism evokes knowledge of a past before it began, and of a future beyond its death. At the other pole, the universe would not have started, or manifested itself, unless it was at some time going to include organisms—just as current will not begin to flow from the positive end of a wire until the negative terminal is secure. The principle is the same, whether it takes the universe billions of years to polarize itself in the organism, or whether it takes the current one second to traverse a wire 186,000 miles long.

I repeat that the difficulty of understanding the organism/environment polarity is psychological. The history and the geographical distribution of the myth are uncertain, but for several thousand years we have been obsessed with a false humility—on the one hand, putting ourselves down as mere "creatures" who came into this world by the whim of God or the fluke of blind forces, and on the other, conceiving ourselves as separate personal egos fighting to control the physical world. We have lacked the real humility of recognizing that we are members of the biosphere, the "harmony of contained conflicts" in which we cannot exist at all without the cooperation of plants, insects, fish, cattle, and bacteria. In the same measure, we have lacked the proper self-respect of recognizing that I, the individual organism, am a structure of such fabulous ingenuity that it calls the whole universe into being. In the act of putting everything at a distance so as to describe and control it, we have orphaned ourselves both from the surrounding world and from our own bodies—leaving "I" as a discontented and alienated spook, anxious, guilty, unrelated, and alone.

We have attained a view of the world and a type of sanity which is dried-out like a rusty beer can on the beach. It is a world of *objects,* of nothing-buts as ordinary as a formica table with chromium fittings. We find it immensely reassuring—except that it won't stay put, and must therefore be defended even at the cost of scouring the whole planet back to a nice clean rock. For life is, after all, a rather messy and gooey accident in our basically geological universe. "If a man's son asks for bread, will he give him a stone?" The answer is probably, "Yes."

Yet this is no quarrel with scientific thinking, which, as of this date, has gone far, far beyond Newtonian billiards and the myth of the Fully Automatic, mechanical universe of mere objects. That was where science really got its start, but in accordance with William Blake's principle that "The fool who *persists* in his folly will become wise," the persistent scientist is the first to realize the obsolescence of old models of the world. Open a good, standard textbook on quantum theory:

... the world cannot be analyzed correctly into distinct parts; instead, it must be regarded as an indivisible unit in which separate parts appear as valid approximations only in the classical [i.e., Newtonian] limit. ... Thus, at the quantum level of accuracy, an object does not have any "intrinsic" properties (for instance, wave or particle) belonging to itself alone; instead, it shares all its properties mutually and indivisibly with the systems with which it interacts. Moreover, because a given object, such as an electron, interacts at different times with different systems that bring out different potentialities, it undergoes ... continual transformation between the various forms (for instance, wave or particle form) in which it can manifest itself.

Although such fluidity and dependence of form on the environment have not been found, before the advent of quantum theory, at the level of elementary particles in physics, they are not uncommon ... in fields, such as biology, which deal with complex systems. Thus, under suitable environmental conditions, a bacterium can develop into a spore stage, which is completely different in structure, and vice versa.[2]

[2]David Bohm, *Quantum Theory*. Prentice-Hall, New Jersey, 1958. pp. 161–62.

Then there is the other, complementary, side of the picture as presented by the eminent biophysicist Erwin Schrödinger:

> It is not possible that this unity of knowledge, feeling and choice which you call *your own* should have sprung into being from nothingness at a given moment not so long ago; rather this knowledge, feeling and choice are essentially eternal and unchangeable and numerically *one* in all men, nay in all sensitive beings. But not in *this* sense—that *you* are a part, a piece, of an eternal, infinite being, an aspect or modification of it, as in Spinoza's pantheism. For we should have the same baffling question: which part, which aspect are *you?* What, objectively, differentiates it from the others? No, but inconceivable as it seems to ordinary reason, you— and all other conscious beings as such—are all in all. Hence this life of yours which you are living is not merely a piece of the entire existence, but is in a certain sense the *whole;* only this whole is not so constituted that it can be surveyed in one single glance.[3]

The universe implies the organism, and each single organism implies the universe—only the "single glance" of our spotlight, narrowed attention, which has been taught to confuse its glimpses with separate "things," must somehow be opened to the full vision, which Schrödinger goes on to suggest:

> Thus you can throw yourself flat on the ground, stretched out upon Mother Earth, with the certain con-

[3]Erwin Schrödinger, *My View of the World.* Cambridge University Press, 1964. pp. 21–22.

viction that you are one with her and she with you. You are as firmly established, as invulnerable as she, indeed a thousand times firmer and more invulnerable. As surely as she will engulf you tomorrow, so surely will she bring you forth anew to new striving and suffering. And not merely 'some day': now, today, every day she is bringing you forth, not *once* but thousands upon thousands of times, just as every day she engulfs you a thousand times over. For eternally and always there is only *now,* one and the same now; the present is the only thing that has no end.[4]

[4]The same, p. 22.

Five

SO WHAT?

$\mathcal{T}$o have spoken of a new vision is to be asked, in the next breath, what good it will do. When you come to think of it, this is astonishing, but it is invariably true in speaking with people brought up in the environment of Protestantism. Catholics, Hindus, Buddhists, Moslems, and Taoists understand that vision, or contemplation, is good in itself, even the supreme good in the sense of the Beatific Vision where all beings are eternally absorbed in the knowledge and love of God. But this possibility makes Protestants nervous, and one of their official prayers asks that those in heaven may be granted "continual growth in thy love and service," because, after all, you can't stop Progress. Even heaven must be a growing community.

The reason is, I suppose, that modern Protestantism

in particular, in its liberal and progressive forms, is the religion most strongly influenced by the mythology of the world of objects, and of man as the separate ego. Man so defined and so experienced is, of course, incapable of pleasure and contentment, let alone creative power. Hoaxed into the illusion of being an independent, responsible source of actions, he cannot understand why what he does never comes up to what he *should* do, for a society which has defined him as separate cannot persuade him to behave as if he really belonged. Thus he feels chronic guilt and makes the most heroic efforts to placate his conscience.

From these efforts come social services, hospitals, peace movements, foreign-aid programs, free education, and the whole philosophy of the welfare state. Yet we are bedeviled by the fact that the more these heroic and admirable enterprises succeed, the more they provoke new and increasingly horrendous problems. For one thing, few of us have ever thought through the problem of what good such enterprises are ultimately supposed to achieve. When we have fed the hungry, clothed the naked, and housed the homeless, what then? Is the object to enable unfortunate people to help those still more unfortunate? To convert Hindus and Africans into a huge *bourgeoisie,* where every Bengali and every Zulu has the privilege of joining our special rat-race, buying appliances on time and a television set to keep him running?

Some years ago a friend of mine was walking through tea plantations near Darjeeling, and noticed one particular group of fields where the bushes were all shriveled. On asking why, it was explained that the owner had felt so sorry for his impoverished workers that he had paid them double. But as a result, they had turned up for work only half the time, which was disastrous in the critical season when the plants have to be tended every day. My friend put this problem to an Indian communist. His solution was to pay them double and compel them to work. He then put it to an American businessman. His solution was to pay them double—and put radios in their homes! No one seemed to understand that those workers valued time for goofing off more than money.

It is hard for compulsive activists to see that the vast social and economic problems of the world cannot be settled by mere effort and technique. The outsider cannot just barge in like Santa Claus and put things to right—especially our kind of outsider who, because he has no sense of belonging in the world, invariably smells like an interferer. He does not really know what he wants, and therefore everyone suspects that there are limitless strings attached to his gifts. For if you know what you want, and will be content with it, you can be trusted. But if you do not know, your desires are limitless and no one can tell how to deal with you. Nothing satisfies an individual incapable of enjoyment. I am not saying that American and European corporations are run by greedy villains who live off the fat of the land at everyone else's expense. The point becomes clear only as one realizes, with compassion and sorrow, that many of our most powerful and wealthy men are miserable dupes and captives in a treadmill, who—with the rarest exceptions—have not the ghost of a notion how to spend and enjoy money.

> *If I had been a Heathen,*
> *I'd have praised the purple vine,*
> *My slaves would dig the vineyards,*
> *And I would drink the wine;*
> *But Higgins is a Heathen,*
> *And his slaves grow lean and grey,*
> *That he may drink some tepid milk*
> *Exactly twice a day.*[1]

The startling truth is that our best efforts for civil rights, international peace, population control, conservation of natural resources, and assistance to the starving of the earth—urgent as they are—will destroy rather than help if made in the present spirit. For, as things stand, we have nothing to give. If our own riches and our own way of life are not enjoyed here, they will not be enjoyed anywhere else. Certainly they will supply the immediate jolt of energy and hope that methedrine, and similar drugs, give in extreme fatigue. But peace can be made only by those who are peaceful, and love can be shown only by those who love. No work of love will flourish out of guilt, fear, or hollowness of heart, just as no valid plans for the future can be made by those who have no capacity for living now.

The separate person is without content, in both senses of the word. He lives perpetually on hope, on looking forward to tomorrow, having been brought up this way from childhood, when his uncomprehending rage at double-binds was propitiated with toys. If you want to find a true folk-religion in our culture, look at the rites

---

[1] G. K. Chesterton, "The Song of the Strange Ascetic," *Collected Poems*. Dodd, Mead, New York, 1932. p. 199.

of Santa Claus. Even before the beginning of Advent, which was supposed to be a three-to-four week fasting period in preparation for the feast, the streets are decorated for Christmas, the shops glitter with tinsel and festive displays of gifts, and public-address systems warble electronic carols so that one is sick to death of *Venite adoremus* long before Christmas Day. Trees are already baubled and illumined in most homes, and as the big buildup proceeds they are surrounded by those shiny packages with shimmering ribbons which look as if they held gifts for princes. By this time Christmas parties have already been held in schools and offices before closing for the actual holiday, so that by Christmas Eve the celebrations have just about blown their top. But there are still those packages under the tree and stockings by the fireplace.

When at last the Day comes the children are frantic. Hardly able to wait for breakfast, and not having slept most of the night, they tear those gold and silver parcels to shreds as if they contained nothing less than the Elixir of Life or the Philosopher's Stone. By noon the living-room looks as if a waste-paper truck had crashed into a dimestore, leaving a wreck of mangled cartons, excelsior, wrapping-paper, and writhing ribbons; neckties, up-ended dolls, half-assembled model railroads, spacesuits, plastic atom-bombs, and scattered chocolate bars; hundreds of tinker-toy pieces, crushed tree ornaments, miniature sports-cars, water-pistols, bottles of whisky, and balloons. An hour later the children are blubbering or screaming, and have to be shooed out-of-doors while the mess is shoved together to make room for Christmas dinner. Thereafter, the Twelve

Days of Christmas are spent with upset stomachs, colds, and influenza, and on New Year's Eve the adults get stoned to forget the whole thing.

Well, it was fun describing it, but the point is that intense expectation fizzled. The girl was gorgeous but the guy was impotent. But since there must be something somewhere, expectation is kindled again to keep us all going for that golden, galuptious goodie at the end of the line. What could it be? The children knew it well until they got caught in the rat-race. One of the best Christmas presents I ever had was a cheap ring with a glass diamond. It was quite incidental—something that came out of a snapper (or cracker) at a party. But I sat down in front of the fireplace with this enchanted object, and turned it to catch the different colors of light which blazed inside it. I knew that I had found the Ring of Solomon, with which he summoned djinns and afrits with wings of brass—and it wasn't that I wanted them to do anything for me, for it was just enough to be in that atmosphere, to watch these magical beings come to life in the flames of the fire, and to feel that I was in touch with the timeless paradise-world.

Now it is symptomatic of our rusty-beer-can type of sanity that our culture produces very few magical objects. Jewelry is slick and uninteresting. Architecture is almost totally bereft of exuberance, obsessed with erecting glass boxes. Children's books are written by serious ladies with three names and no imagination, and as for comics, have you ever looked at the furniture in Dagwood's home? The potentially magical ceremonies of the Catholic Church are either gabbled away at top speed, or rationalized with the aid of a commentator. Drama or ritual in everyday behavior is considered affectation and bad form, and manners have become indistinguishable from mannerisms—where they exist at all. We produce nothing comparable to the great Oriental carpets, Persian glass, tiles, and illuminated books, Arabian leatherwork, Spanish marquetry, Hindu textiles, Chinese porcelain and embroidery, Japanese lacquer and brocade, French tapestries, or Inca jewelry. (Though, incidentally, there are certain rather small electronic devices that come unwittingly close to fine jewels.)

The reason is not just that we are too much in a hurry and have no sense of the present; not just that we cannot afford the type of labor that such things would now involve, nor just that we prefer money to materials. The reason is that we have scrubbed the world clean of magic. We have lost even the vision of paradise, so that our artists and craftsmen can no longer discern its forms. This is the price that must be paid for attempting to control the world from the standpoint of an "I" for whom everything that can be experienced is a foreign object and a nothing-but.

It would be sentimental and impossible to go back. Children are in touch with paradise to the extent that they have not fully learned the ego-trick, and the same is true of cultures which, by our standards, are more "primitive" and—by analogy—childlike. If, then, after understanding, at least in theory, that the ego-trick is a hoax and that, beneath everything, "I" and "universe" are one, you ask, "So what? What is the next step, the practical application?"—I will answer that the absolutely vital thing is to consolidate your understanding, to become capable of enjoyment, of living in the present, and of the discipline which this involves. Without this you have nothing to give—to the cause of peace or of racial integration, to starving Hindus and Chinese, or even to your closest friends. Without this, all social concern will be muddlesome meddling, and all work for the future will be planned disaster.

But the way is not back. Just as science overcame its purely atomistic and mechanical view of the world through *more* science, the ego-trick must be overcome through intensified self-consciousness. For there is no way of getting rid of the feeling of separateness by a so-called "act of will," by trying to forget yourself, or by getting absorbed in some other interest. This is why moralistic preaching is such a failure: it breeds only cunning hypocrites—people sermonized into shame, guilt, or fear, who thereupon force themselves to behave as if they actually loved others, so that their "virtues" are often more destructive, and arouse more resentment, than their "vices." A British social service project, run by earnest and rather formidable ladies, called the Charity Organization Society—C.O.S. for short—used to be known among the poor as "Cringe or Starve."

The Taoist philosopher Chuang-tzu described such efforts to be ego-less as "beating a drum in search of a fugitive," or, as we would put it, driving to a police raid with sirens on. Or, as the Hindus say, it is like trying *not* to think of a monkey while taking medicine, on the basis of the popular superstition that thinking of a monkey will make the medicine ineffective. All that such efforts can teach us is that they do not work, for the more we try to behave without greed or fear, the more we realize that we are doing this for greedy or fearful reasons. Saints have always declared themselves as abject sinners—through recognition that their aspiration to be saintly is motivated by the worst of all sins, spiritual pride, the desire to admire oneself as a supreme success in the art of love and unselfishness. And beneath this lies a bottomless pit of vicious circles: the game, "I am more penitent that you" or "My pride in my humility is worse than yours." Is there any way *not* to be involved in some kind of one-upmanship? "I am less of a one-upman than you." "I am a worse one-upman than you." "I realize more clearly than you that everything we do is one-upmanship." The ego-trick seems to reaffirm itself endlessly in posture after posture.

But as I pursue these games—as I become more conscious of being conscious, more aware that I am unable to define myself as being *up* without you (or something other than myself) being *down*—I see vividly that I *depend* on your being down for my being up. I would never be able to know that I belong to the in-group of "nice" or "saved" people without the assistance of an out-group of "nasty" or "damned" people. How can any in-group maintain its collective ego without relishing dinner-table discussions about the ghastly conduct of outsiders? The very identity of racist Southerners depends upon contrasting themselves with those dirty black "nigras." But, conversely, the out-groups feel that they are really and truly "in," and nourish their collective ego with relishingly indignant conversation about squares, Ofays, Wasps, Philistines, and the blasted *bour-*

geoisie. Even Saint Thomas Aquinas let it out that part of the blessedness of the saints in Heaven was that they could look over the battlements and enjoy the "proper justice" of the sinners squirming in Hell. All winners need losers; all saints need sinners; all sages need fools—that is, so long as the major kick in life is to "amount to something" or to "be someone" as a particular and separate godlet.

But I define myself in terms of you; I know myself only in terms of what is "other," no matter whether I see the "other" as below me or above me in any ladder of values. If above, I enjoy the kick of self-pity; if below, I enjoy the kick of pride. I being I goeswith you being you. Thus, as a great Hassidic rabbi put it, "If I am I because you are you, and if you are you because I am I, then I am not I, and you are not you." Instead we are both something in common between what Martin Buber has called I-and-Thou and I-and-It—the magnet itself which lies between the poles, between I myself and everything sensed as other.

There it is, a theoretically undeniable fact. But the question is how to get over the *sensation* of being locked out from everything "other," of being only oneself—an organism flung into unavoidable competition and conflict with almost every "object" in its experience. There are innumerable recipes for this project, almost all of which have something to recommend them. There are the practices of yoga meditation, dervish dancing, psychotherapy, Zen Buddhism, Ignatian, Salesian, and Hesychast methods of "prayer," the use of consciousness-changing chemicals such as LSD and mescaline, psychodrama, group dynamics, sensory-awareness techniques, Quakerism, Gurdjieff exercises, relaxation therapies, the Alexander method, autogenic training, and self-hypnosis. The difficulty with every one of these disciplines is that the moment you are seriously involved, you find yourself boxed in some special ingroup which defines itself, often with the most elegant subtlety, by the exclusion of an out-group. In this way, every religion or cult is self-defeating, and this is equally true of projects which define themselves as non-religions or universally inclusive religions, playing the game of "I am less exclusive than you."

It is thus that religions and non-religions—all established in the name of brotherhood and universal love—are invariably divisive and quarrelsome. What, for example, is more quarrelsome—in practical politics—than the project for a truly classless and democratic society? Yet the historical origin of this movement is mystical. It goes back to Jesus and Saint Paul, to Eckhart and Tauler, to the Anabaptists, Levelers, and Brothers of the Free Spirit, and their insistence that all men are equal in the sight of God. It seems almost as if to be is to quarrel, or at least to differ, to be in contrast with something else. If so, whoever does not put up a fight has no identity; whoever is not self-ish has no self. Nothing unites a community so much as common cause against an external enemy, yet, in the same moment, that enemy becomes the essential support of social unity. Therefore larger societies require larger enemies, bringing us in due course to the perilous point of our present situation, where the world is virtually divided into two huge camps. But if high officers on both sides have any intelligence at all, they make a secret agreement to contain the conflict: to call each other the worst names, but to refrain from dropping bombs. Or, if they insist that there must be some fighting to keep armies in trim, they restrict it to local conflicts in "unimportant" countries. Voltaire should have said that if the Devil did not exist, it would be necessary to invent him.

Nevertheless, the more it becomes clear that to be is to quarrel and to pursue self-interest, the more you are compelled to recognize your need for enemies to support you. In the same way, the more resolutely you plumb the question "Who or what am I?"—the more unavoidable is the realization that you are nothing at all apart from everything *else.* Yet again, the more you strive for some kind of perfection or mastery—in morals, in art, or in spirituality—the more you see that you are playing a rarified and lofty form of the old ego-game, and that your attainment of any height is apparent to yourself and to others only by contrast with someone else's depth or failure.

This understanding is at first paralyzing. You are in a trap—in the worst of all double-binds—seeing that any direction you may take will imply, and so evoke, its opposite. Decide to be a Christ, and there will be a Judas to betray you and a mob to crucify you. Decide to be a devil, and men will unite against you in the closest brotherly love. Your first reaction may be simply, "To hell with it!" The only course may seem to be to forget the whole effort and become absorbed in trivialities, or to check out of the game by suicide or psychosis, and spend the rest of your days blabbering in an asylum.

But there is another possibility. Instead of checking

out, let us ask what the trap means. What is implied in finding yourself paralyzed, unable to escape from a game in which all the rules are double-binds and all moves self-defeating? Surely this is a deep and intense experience of the same double-bind that was placed upon you in infancy, when the community told you that you *must* be free, responsible, and loving, and when you were helplessly defined as an independent agent. The sense of paralysis is therefore the dawning realization that this is nonsense and that your independent ego is *a* fiction. It simply isn't there, either to do anything or to be pushed around by external forces, to change things or to submit to change. The sense of "I," which should have been identified with the whole universe of your experience, was instead cut off and isolated as a detached observer of that universe. In the preceding chapter we saw that this unity of organism and environment is a physical fact. But when you know for sure that your separate ego is a fiction, you actually *feel* yourself *as* the whole process and pattern of life. Experience and experiencer become one experiencing, known and knower one knowing.

Each organism experiences this from a different standpoint and in a different way, for each organism is the universe experiencing itself in endless variety. One need not, then, fall into the trap which this experience holds for believers in an external, all-powerful God—the temptation to feel "I am God" in that sense, and to expect to be worshipped and obeyed by all other organisms.

Remember, above all, that an experience of this kind cannot be forced or made to happen by any act of your fictitious "will," except insofar as repeated efforts to be one-up on the universe may eventually reveal their futility. Don't try to get rid of the ego-sensation. Take it, so long as it lasts, as a feature or play of the total process—like a cloud or wave, or like feeling warm or cold, or anything else that happens of itself. Getting rid of one's ego is the last resort of invincible egoism! It simply confirms and strengthens the reality of the feeling. But when this feeling of separateness is approached and accepted like any other sensation, it evaporates like the mirage that it is.

This is why I am not overly enthusiastic about the various "spiritual exercises" in meditation or yoga which some consider essential for release from the ego. For when practiced *in order* to "get" some kind of spiritual illumination or awakening, they strengthen the fallacy that the ego can toss itself away by a tug at its own bootstraps. But there is nothing wrong with meditating just to meditate, in the same way that you listen to music just for the music. If you go to concerts to "get culture" or to improve your mind, you will sit there as deaf as a doorpost.

If, then, you ask me *how* to get beyond the ego-feeling, I shall ask you *why* you want to get there. If you give me the honest answer, which is that your ego will feel better in the "higher spiritual status" of self-transcendence, you will thus realize that you—as ego—are a fake. You will feel like an onion: skin after skin, subterfuge after subterfuge, is pulled off to find no kernel at the center. Which is the whole point: to find out that the ego is indeed a fake—a wall of defense around a wall of defense . . . around nothing. You can't even want to get rid of it, nor yet want to want to.

Understanding this, you will see that the ego is exactly what it pretends it isn't. Far from being the free center of personality, it is an automatic mechanism implanted since childhood by social authority, with—perhaps—a touch of heredity thrown in. This may give you the temporary feeling of being a zombie or a puppet dancing irresponsibly on strings that lead away to unknown forces. At this point, the ego may reassert itself with the insidious "I-can't-help-myself" play in which the ego splits itself in two and pretends that it is its own victim. "See, I'm only a bundle of conditioned reflexes, so you mustn't get angry with me for acting just as I feel." (To which the answer could be, "Well, we're just zombies too, so you shouldn't complain if we get angry.")

But who is it that *mustn't* get angry or *shouldn't* complain, as if there were still some choice in the matter? The ego is still surviving as the "I" which must passively endure the automatic behavior of "myself" and others—again, as if there were some choice which the witnessing self can make between putting up with things and attacking them violently. What has happened is that the frustrated ego has withdrawn into its last stronghold of independence, retaining its identity as a mere watcher, or sufferer, of all that goes on. Here it pities itself or consoles itself as a puppet of fate.

But if this is seen as yet another subterfuge, we are close to the final showdown. A line of separation is now drawn between everything that happens to me, including my own feelings, on the one side, and on the other, I myself as the conscious witness. Isn't it easy to see that this line is imaginary, and that it, and the witness behind it, are the same old faking process automatically learned in childhood? The same old cleft between the knower and the known? The same old split between the organism/environment and the organism's feedback, or self-conscious mechanism? If, then, there is no choice in what happens to me, on one side of the line, there is equally no choice on the other, on the witnessing side, as to whether I should accept what happens or reject it. I accept, I reject, I witness just as automatically as things happen or as my emotions reflect my physiological chemistry.

Yet in this moment when one seems about to become a really total zombie, the whole thing blows up. For there is no fate unless there is someone or something to be fated. There is no trap without someone to be caught. There is, indeed, no compulsion unless there is also freedom of choice, for the sensation of behaving involuntarily is known only by contrast with that of behaving voluntarily. Thus when the line between myself and what happens to me is dissolved and there is no stronghold left for an ego even as a passive witness, I find myself not *in* a world but *as* a world which is neither compulsive nor capricious. What happens is neither automatic nor arbitrary: it just happens, and all happenings are mutually interdependent in a way that seems unbelievably harmonious. Every this goes with every that. Without others there is no self, and without somewhere else there is no here, so that—in this sense—self is other and here is there.

When this new sensation of self arises, it is at once exhilarating and a little disconcerting. It is like the moment when you first got the knack of swimming or riding a bicycle. There is the feeling that you are not doing it yourself, but that it is somehow happening on its own, and you wonder whether you will lose it—as indeed you may if you try forcibly to hold on to it. In immediate contrast to the old feeling, there is indeed a certain passivity to the sensation, as if you were a leaf blown along by the wind, until you realize that you are both the leaf and the wind. The world outside your skin is just as much you as the world inside: they move together inseparably, and at first you feel a little out of control because the world outside is so much vaster than the world inside. Yet you soon discover that you are able to go ahead with ordinary activities—to work and make decisions as ever, though somehow this is less of a drag. Your body is no longer a corpse which the ego has to animate and lug around. There is a feeling of the ground holding you up, and of hills lifting you when you climb them. Air breathes itself in and out of your lungs, and instead of looking and listening, light and sound come to you on their own. Eyes see and ears hear as wind blows and water flows. All space becomes your mind. Time carries you along like a river, but never flows out of the present: the more it goes, the more it stays, and you no longer have to fight or kill it.

You do not ask what is the value, or what is the use, of this feeling. Of what use is the universe? What is the practical application of a million galaxies? Yet just because it has no use, it has a use—which may sound like a paradox, but is not. What, for instance, is the use of playing music? If you play to make money, to outdo some other artist, to be a person of culture, or to improve your mind, you are not really playing—for your mind is not on the music. You don't swing. When you come to think of it, playing or listening to music is a pure luxury, an addiction, a waste of valuable time and money for nothing more than making elaborate patterns of sound. Yet what would we think of a society which had no place for music, which did not allow for dancing, or for any activity not directly involved with the practical problems of survival? Obviously, such a society would be surviving to no purpose—unless it could somehow make a delight out of the "essential tasks" of farming, building, soldiering, manufacturing, or cooking. But in that moment the goal of survival is forgotten. The tasks are being done for their own sake, whereupon farms begin to look like gardens, sensible living-boxes sprout interesting roofs and mysterious ornaments, arms are engraved with curious patterns, carpenters take time to "finish" their work, and cooks become gourmets.

A Chinese philosophical work called *The Secret of the Golden Flower* says that "when purpose has been used to achieve purposelessness, the thing has been grasped." For a society surviving to no purpose is one that makes no provision for purposeless behavior—that is, for actions not directly aimed at survival, which fulfill themselves in being done in the present and do not necessarily imply some future reward. But indirectly and unintentionally, such behavior is useful for survival because it gives a point to surviving—not, however, when pursued for that reason. To play so as to be relaxed and refreshed for work is not to play, and no work is well and finely done unless it, too, is a form of play.

To be released from the "You *must* survive" double-bind is to see that life is at root playing. The difficulty in understanding this is that the idea of "play" has two distinct meanings which are often confused. On the one hand, to do something *only* or *merely* in play, is to be trivial and insincere, and here we should use the word "toying" instead of "playing." But if some woman should say to me, "I love you," would it be right to answer, "Are you serious, or are you just playing with me?" After all, if this relationship is to flourish, I very much hope that she is *not* serious and that she *will* play with me. No, the better question would be, "Are you sincere, or are you just toying with me?" Sincerity is better than seriousness, for who wants to be loved gravely? Thus, on the other hand, there is a form of playing which is not trivial at all, as when Segovia plays the guitar or Sir Laurence Olivier plays the part of Hamlet, or, obviously, when someone plays the organ in church. In this sense of the word Saint Gregory Nazianzen could say of the Logos, the creative wisdom of God:

> *For the Logos on high plays,*
> *stirring the whole cosmos back and forth, as he wills,*
> *into shapes of every kind.*

And, at the other end of the earth, the Japanese Zen master Hakuin:

> *In singing and dancing is the voice of the Law.*

So, too, in the Vedanta the whole world is seen as the *lila* and the *maya* of the Self, the first word meaning "play" and the second having the complex sense of illusion (from the Latin *ludere,* to play) magic, creative power, art, and measuring—as when one dances or draws a design to a certain measure. From this point of view the universe in general and playing in particular are, in a special sense, "meaningless": that is, they do not—like words and symbols—signify or point to something beyond themselves, just as a Mozart sonata conveys no moral or social message and does not try to suggest the natural sounds of wind, thunder, or birdsong. When I make the sound "water," you know what I mean. But what does this whole situation mean—I making the sound and your understanding it? What is the meaning of a pelican, a sunflower, a sea urchin, a mottled stone, or a galaxy? Or of $a + b = b + a$? They are all patterns, dancing patterns of light and sound, water and fire, rhythm and vibration, electricity and spacetime, going like

> *Thrummular, thrummular thrilp,*
> *Hum lipsible, lipsible lilp;*
> *Dim thricken mithrummy,*
> *Lumgumptulous hummy,*
> *Stormgurgle umbumdular bilp.*

Or, in the famous words of Sir Arthur Eddington about the nature of electrons:

> We see the atoms with their girdles of circulating electrons darting hither and thither, colliding and rebounding. Free electrons torn from the girdles hurry away a hundred times faster, curving sharply round the atoms with side-slips and hairbreadth escapes. . . . The spectacle is so fascinating that we have perhaps for-

gotten that there was a time when we wanted to be told what an electron is. The question was never answered. . . . *Something unknown is doing we don't know what*—that is what our theory amounts to. It does not sound a particularly illuminating theory. I have read something like it elsewhere:

> The slithy toves
> Did gyre and gimble in the wabe.

There is the same suggestion of activity. There is the same indefiniteness as to the nature of the activity and of what it is that is acting.[2]

The point is that "spectacle is so fascinating." For the world is a spell (in Latin, *fascinum*), an enchantment (being thrilled by a chant), an amazement (being lost in a maze), an arabesque of such stunning rhythm and a plot so intriguing that we are drawn by its web into a state of involvement where we forget that it is a game. We become fascinated to the point where the cheering and the booing are transformed into intense love and hate, or delight and terror, ecstatic orgasm or screaming meemies. All made out of on-and-off or black-and-white, pulsed, stuttered, diagrammed mosaiced, syncopated, shaded, jolted, tangoed, and lilted through all possible measures and dimensions. It is simultaneously the purest nonsense and the utmost artistry.

Listen intently to a voice singing without words. It may charm you into crying, force you to dance, fill you with rage, or make you jump for joy. You can't tell where the music ends and the emotions begin, for the

---

[2] *The Nature of the Physical World.* J. M. Dent, London, 1935. pp. 280–81.

whole thing is a kind of music—the voice playing on your nerves as the breath plays on a flute. All experience is just that, except that its music has many more dimensions than sound. It vibrates in the dimensions of sight, touch, taste, and smell, and in the intellectual dimension of symbols and words—all evoking and playing upon each other. But at root—and this is a negative way of saying something highly positive—it is nothing more than the mysterious utterance of the old man of Spithead, who opened the window and said:

> Fill jomble, fill jumble,
> Fill rumble-come-tumble.

Bach states it more elegantly, but with just as little external meaning:

Once you have seen this you can return to the world of practical affairs with a new spirit. You have seen that the universe is at root a magical illusion and a fabulous game, and that there is no separate "you" to get something out of it, as if life were a bank to be robbed. The only real "you" is the one that comes and goes, manifests and withdraws itself eternally in and as every conscious being. For "you" is the universe looking at itself from billions of points of view, points that come and go so that the vision is forever new. What we see as death, empty space, or nothingness is only the trough between the crests of this endlessly waving ocean. It is all part of the illusion that there should seem to be something to be gained in the future, and that there is an urgent necessity to go on and on until we get it. Yet just as there is no time but the present, and no one except the all-and-everything, there is never anything to be gained—though the zest of the game is to pretend that there is.

Anyone who brags about knowing this doesn't understand it, for he is only using the theory as a trick to maintain his illusion of separateness, a gimmick in a game of spiritual one-upmanship. Moreover, such bragging is deeply offensive to those who do not understand, and who honestly believe themselves to be lonely, individual spirits in a desperate and agonizing struggle for life. For all such there must be deep and unpatronizing compassion, even a special kind of reverence and respect, because, after all, in them the Self is playing its most far-out and daring game—the game of having lost Itself completely and of being in danger of some total and irremediable disaster. This is why Hindus do not shake hands on meeting, but put their palms together and bow in a gesture of reverence, honoring the Godhead in the stranger.

And do not suppose that this understanding will transform you all at once into a model of virtue. I have never yet met a saint or sage who did not have some human frailties. For so long as you manifest yourself in human or animal form, you must eat at the expense of other life and accept the limitations of your particular organism, which fire will still burn and wherein danger will still secrete adrenalin. The morality that goes with this understanding is, above all, the frank recognition of your dependence upon enemies, underlings, out-groups, and, indeed, upon all other forms of life what-soever. Involved as you may be in the conflicts and competitive games of practical life, you will never again be able to indulge in the illusion that the "offensive other" is all in the wrong, and could or should be wiped out. This will give you the priceless ability of being able to contain conflicts so that they do not get out-of-hand, of being willing to compromise and adapt, of playing, yes, but playing it cool. This is what is called "honor among thieves," for the really dangerous people are those who do not recognize that they are thieves—the unfortunates who play the role of the "good guys" with such blind zeal that they are unconscious of any in-debtedness to the "bad guys" who support their status. To paraphrase the Gospel, "Love your competitors, and pray for those who undercut your prices." You would be nowhere at all without them.

The political and personal morality of the West, es-pecially in the United States, is—for lack of this sense—utterly schizophrenic. It is a monstrous combination of uncompromising idealism and unscrupulous gangster-ism, and thus devoid of the humor and humaneness which enables confessed rascals to sit down together and work out reasonable deals. No one can be moral—that is, no one can harmonize contained conflicts—without coming to a working arrangement between the angel in himself and the devil in himself, between his rose above and his manure below. The two forces or tendencies are mutually interdependent, and the game is a working game just so long as the angel is winning, but does not win, and the devil is losing, but is never lost. (The game doesn't work in reverse, just as the ocean doesn't work with wave-crests down and troughs up.)

It is most important that this be understood by those concerned with civil rights, international peace, and the restraint of nuclear weapons. These are most undoubtedly causes to be backed with full vigor, but never in a spirit which fails to honor the opposition, or which regards it as entirely evil or insane. It is not without reason that the formal rules of boxing, judo, fencing, and even dueling require that the combatants salute each other before the engagement. In any foreseeable future there are going to be thousands and thousands of people who detest and abominate Negroes, communists, Russians, Chinese, Jews, Catholics, beatniks, homosexuals, and "dope-fiends." These hatreds are not going to be healed, but only inflamed, by insulting those who feel them, and the abusive labels with which we plaster them—squares, fascists, rightists, know-nothings—may well become the proud badges and symbols around which they will rally and consolidate themselves. Nor will it do to confront the opposition in public with polite and non-violent sit-ins and demonstrations, while boosting our collective ego by insulting them in private. If we want justice for minorities and cooled wars with our natural enemies, whether human or nonhuman, we must first come to terms with the minority and the enemy in ourselves and in our own hearts, for the rascal is there as much as anywhere in the "external" world—especially when you realize that the world

outside your skin is as much yourself as the world inside. For want of this awareness, no one can be more
belligerent than a pacifist on the rampage, or more mil-
itantly nationalistic than an anti-imperialist.

You may, indeed, argue that this is asking too much.
You may resort to the old alibi that the task of "changing human nature" is too arduous and too slow, and
that what we need is immediate and massive action.
Obviously, it takes discipline to make any radical
change in one's own behavior patterns, and psychotherapy can drag on for years and years. But this is not
my suggestion. Does it really take any considerable time
or effort just to *understand* that you depend on enemies
and outsiders to define yourself, and that without some
opposition you would be lost? To see this is to acquire,
almost instantly, the virtue of humor, and humor and
self-righteousness are mutually exclusive. Humor is the
twinkle in the eye of a just judge, who knows that he
is *also* the felon in the dock. How could he be sitting
there in stately judgment, being addressed as "Your
Honor" or "Mi Lud," without those poor bastards being dragged before him day after day? It does not un-
dermine his work and his function to recognize this. He
plays the role of judge all the better for realizing that
on the next turn of the Wheel of Fortune he may be the
accused, and that if *all* the truth were known, he would
be standing there now.

If this is cynicism, it is at least loving cynicism—an
attitude and an atmosphere that cools off human conflicts more effectively than any amount of physical or
moral violence. For it recognizes that the real goodness
of human nature is its peculiar balance of love and self-

ishness, reason and passion, spirituality and sensuality, mysticism and materialism, in which the positive pole has always a slight edge over the negative. (Were it otherwise, and the two were equally balanced, life would come to a total stalemate and standstill.) Thus when the two poles, good and bad, forget their interdependence and try to obliterate each other, man becomes subhuman—the implacable crusader or the cold, sadistic thug. It is not for man to be either an angel or a devil, and the would-be angels should realize that, as their ambition succeeds, they evoke hordes of devils to keep the balance. This was the lesson of Prohibition, as of all other attempts to enforce purely angelic behavior, or to pluck out evil root and branch.

It comes, then, to this: that to be "viable," livable, or merely practical, life must be lived as a game—and the "must" here expresses a condition, not a commandment. It must be lived in the spirit of play rather than work, and the conflicts which it involves must be carried on in the realization that no species, or party to a game, can survive without its natural antagonists, its beloved enemies, its indispensable opponents. For to "love your enemies" is to love them *as* enemies; it is not necessarily a clever device for winning them over to your own side. The lion lies down with the lamb in paradise, but not on earth—"paradise" being the tacit, off-stage level where, behind the scenes, all conflicting parties recognize their interdependence, and, through this recognition, are able to keep their conflicts within bounds. This recognition is the absolutely essential chivalry which must set the limits within all warfare, with human and non-human enemies alike, for chivalry is the debonair spirit of the knight who "plays with his life" in the knowledge that even mortal combat is a game.

No one who has been hoaxed into the belief that he is nothing but his ego, or nothing but his individual organism, can be chivalrous, let alone a civilized, sensitive, and intelligent member of the cosmos.

But to be lived this way, the life-game has to be purged of self-contradictory rules. This, and not some kind of moral effort, is the way out of the hoax of separateness. Thus when a game sets the players an impossible and not simply difficult task, it comes quickly to the point where it is no longer worth playing. There is no way of observing a rule set in the form of a double-bind—that is, a two-part rule whose parts are mutually exclusive. No one can be compelled to behave freely or forced to act independently. Yet whole cultures and civilizations have befuddled themselves with this kind of nonsense, and, through failing to spot the self-contradiction, their members have been haunted all through their lives by the sense that individual existence is a problem and a predicament—a form of nature doomed to perpetual frustration. The sense of ego is at root a discomfort and a bore, and nothing shows it more clearly than such everyday phrases as: "I need to get away from myself" or "You should find something to take you out of yourself" or "I read to forget myself." Get lost! Hence the fanaticisms and intoxications—religious, political, and sexual, the Nazis, the Klan, Hell's Angels, the Circus Maximus, the dreary fascination of the TV screen, witch-burnings, Mickey Spillane and James Bond, pachinko parlors, alcoholic stupors, revivals, tabloid newspapers, and juvenile gangs—all of which, as things stand, are the necessary safety-values and palliatives for human beings whose very existence is defined in self-contradictory and self-defeating terms.

Finally, the game of life as Western man has been "playing" it for the past century needs less emphasis on practicality, results, progress, and aggression. This is why I am discussing *vision,* and keeping off the subject of justifying the vision in terms of its practical applications and consequences. Whatever may be true for the Chinese and the Hindus, it is timely for *us* to recognize that the future is an ever-retreating mirage, and to switch our immense energy and technical skill to contemplation instead of action. However much we may now disagree with Aristotle's logic and his metaphors, he must still be respected for reminding us that the goal of action is always contemplation—knowing and being rather than seeking and becoming.

As it is, we are merely bolting our lives—gulping down undigested experiences as fast as we can stuff them in—because awareness of our own existence is so superficial and so narrow that nothing seems to us more boring than simple being. If I ask you what you did, saw, heard, smelled, touched, and tasted yesterday, I am likely to get nothing more than the thin, sketchy outline of the few things that you noticed, and of those only what you thought worth remembering. Is it surprising that an existence so experienced seems so empty and bare that its hunger for an infinite future is insatiable? But suppose you could answer, "It would take me forever to tell you, and I am much too interested in what's happening now." How is it possible that a being with such sensitive jewels as the eyes, such enchanted musical instruments as the ears, and such a fabulous arabesque of nerves as the brain can experience itself as anything less than a god? And, when you consider that this incalculably subtle organism is inseparable from the still more marvelous patterns of its environment—from the minutest electrical designs to the whole company of the galaxies—how is it conceivable that this incarnation of all eternity can be bored with being?

Six

IT

*J*ust as true humor is laughter at oneself, true humanity is knowledge of oneself. Other creatures may love and laugh, talk and think, but it seems to be the special peculiarity of human beings that they reflect: they think about thinking and know that they know. This, like other feedback systems, may lead to vicious circles and confusions if improperly managed, but self-awareness makes human experience resonant. It imparts that simultaneous "echo" to all that we think and feel as the box of a violin reverberates with the sound of the strings. It gives depth and volume to what would otherwise be shallow and flat.

Self-knowledge leads to wonder, and wonder to curiosity and investigation, so that nothing interests people more than people, even if only one's own person. Every intelligent individual wants to know what makes him tick, and yet is at once fascinated and frustrated by the fact that oneself is the most difficult of all things to know. For the human organism is, apparently, the most complex of all organisms, and while one has the advantage of knowing one's own organism so intimately—from the inside—there is also the disadvantage of being so close to it that one can never quite get at it. Nothing so eludes conscious inspection as consciousness itself. This is why the root of consciousness has been called, paradoxically, the unconscious.

The people we are tempted to call clods and boors are just those who seem to find nothing fascinating in being human; their humanity is incomplete, for it has never astonished them. There is also something incomplete about those who find nothing fascinating in *being*. You may say that this is a philosopher's professional prejudice—that people are defective who lack a sense of the metaphysical. But anyone who thinks at all must be a philosopher—a good one or a bad one—because it is impossible to think without premises, without basic (and in this sense, metaphysical) assumptions about what is sensible, what is the good life, what is beauty, and what is pleasure. To hold such assumptions, consciously or unconsciously, is to philosophize. The self-styled practical man of affairs who pooh-poohs philosophy as a lot of windy notions is himself a pragmatist or a positivist, and a bad one at that, since he has given no thought to his position.

If the human organism is fascinating, the environment which accompanies it is equally so—and not merely as a collection of particular things and events. Chemistry, biology, geology, and astronomy are special fascinations with the details of our environment, but metaphysics is fascination with the whole thing. I find it almost impossible to imagine a sensitive human being bereft of metaphysical wonder, a person who does not have that marvelous urge to ask a question that cannot quite be formulated. If, as we have been arguing, the only real atom—as de Chardin put it—is the universe, and the only real thing is everything, then what is it?

Yet the moment I have asked this question, I must question the question. What sort of answer could such a question have? Ordinarily, one answers the question "What is it?" by putting the designated thing or event into a class—animal, vegetable, or mineral, solid, liquid, or gas, running, jumping, or walking. But what class will fit *every*thing? What can possibly be said about everything? To define is to limit, to set boundaries, to compare and to contrast, and for this reason the universe, the all, seems to defy definition. At this point, the mind runs into an apparently absolute limitation, and one may well argue that it is therefore a misuse of the mind to ask such a question. Just as no one in his senses would look for the morning news in a dictionary, no one should use speaking and thinking to find out what cannot be spoken or thought. Logically, then, the question, "What is everything?" has no meaning, even though it seems to be profound. As Wittgenstein suggested, people who ask such questions may have a disorder of the intellect which can be cured by philosophical therapy. To "do philosophy," as he put it, is to think about thinking in such a way that we can distinguish real thinking from nonsense.

But this neat logic does not get rid of the urge to know which expresses itself—however ineptly—in the question. As I said at the beginning, it is just unbelievably odd that anything is happening at all. Yet how am I to express this feeling in the form of a sensible question which could have a satisfactory answer? The point is, perhaps, that I am not looking for a *verbal* answer, just as when I ask for a kiss, I do not want a piece of paper with "A kiss" written on it. It is rather that metaphysical wonder looks for an experience, a vision, a revelation which will explain, without words, why there is the universe, and what it is—much as the act of loving explains why we are male and female.

It could be said, then, that the best answer to "What is everything?" is "Look and see!" But the question almost always implies a search for something *basic* to everything, for an underlying unity which our ordinary thinking and feeling do not grasp. Thought and sensation are analytical and selective, and thus present the world as no more than a multiplicity of things and events. Man has, however, a "metaphysical instinct" which apparent multiplicity does not satisfy.

What guarantee is there that the five senses, taken together, do cover the whole of possible experience? They cover simply our actual experience, our human knowledge of facts or events. There are gaps between the fingers; there are gaps between the senses. In these gaps is the darkness which hides the connection between things. . . . This darkness is the source of our vague fears and anxieties, but also the home of the gods. They alone see the connections, the total relevance of everything that happens; that which now comes to us in bits and pieces, the "accidents" which exist only in our heads, in our limited perceptions.[1]

Man is therefore intuitively certain that the entire multitude of things and events is "on" or "in" something as reflections are on a mirror, sounds on a diaphragm, lights and colors in a diamond, or the words and music of a song in the singer. This is perhaps because man is himself a unified organism, and that if things and events are "on" anything at all, they are on his nervous system. Yet there is obviously more than one nervous system, and what are all nervous systems on? Each other?

This mysterious something has been called God, the Absolute, Nature, Substance, Energy, Space, Ether, Mind, Being, the Void, the Infinite—names and ideas which shift in popularity and respectability with the winds of intellectual fashion, of considering the universe intelligent or stupid, superhuman or subhuman, specific or vague. All of them might be dismissed as nonsense-noises if the notion of an underlying Ground or Being were no more than a product of intellectual speculation. But these names are often used to designate the content of a vivid and almost sensorily concrete experience—the "unitive" experience of the mystic, which, with secondary variations, is found in almost all cultures at all times. This experience is the transformed

[1]Idris Parry, "Kafka, Rilke, and Rumpelstiltskin." *The Listener.* British Broadcasting Corporation, London, December 2, 1965. p. 895.

sense of self which I was discussing in the previous chapter, though in "naturalistic" terms, purified of all hocus-pocus about mind, soul, spirit, and other intellectually gaseous words.

Despite the universality of this experience and the impressive regularity with which it is described in the same general way,[2] tough-minded types regard it as a commonly recurring hallucination with characteristic symptoms, like paranoia, which adds nothing to our information about the physical universe. Just as we cannot say anything about everything, so, they argue, one cannot feel or experience anything about everything. For all our senses are selective. We experience by contrast just as we think by contrast. To experience something underlying *all* experiences would thus be like seeing sight itself, as something common to everything seen. In terms of what color, what shape—other than all mutually contrasting colors and shapes—could we see sight itself?

Yet metaphysics, like philosophy as a whole, is not something which can simply be cured or abandoned, as if it were an intellectual disease. The most antimetaphysical philosophers have, in fact, a tacit metaphysics of their own, which lurks behind the assertion that all experience and all knowledge must be of classes, and of contrasts and comparisons between them. To put it in the simplest way, they will allow that I can know and speak sensibly about something white, since I know

---

[2]For which the reader is directed to such works in the Bibliography as Bucke's *Cosmic Consciousness,* James's *Varieties of Religious Experience,* and Johnson's *Watcher on the Hills.*

white by contrast with black, and by comparison with red, orange, yellow, green, blue, indigo, and violet. They will allow meaningful statements about dogs and cats, because they are organic as distinct from inorganic, mammals as distinct from marsupials, and, though frisky, have clearly defined boundaries which demark them from the whole word of non-dogs and non-cats.

But the underlying assumption, that all knowledge is in terms of contrasts, is as metaphysical as an assumption can be. Put it in another way: "All knowledge is a recognition of the mutual relations between sense-experiences and/or things and events." This comes perilously close to being a meaningful statement about everything. "All things are known by their differences from and likenesses to each other." Backed up into this position, the antimetaphysician can be carried, albeit with screams of protest, to an even deeper metaphysical level.

Grant that the statement "Everything is energy" conveys no more information than "Everything is everything." To describe energy, I must differentiate it from non-energy, or from mass, and thus if "everything" is to include non-energy—mass, space, or whatever—it will not only be uninformative but also nonsense to say that everything is energy. If, then, we are going to insist that energy can be known and described only by contrast with non-energy, this is virtually the same as saying that energy (or motion) is manifested—or simply, exists—only by contrast with something relatively inert. But in this event, energy depends on the inert for being energetic, and the inert depends on the energetic for being inert. This relativity, or interdependence, of the two is as close to a metaphysical unity underlying differences as anyone could wish.

I have sometimes thought that all philosophical disputes could be reduced to an argument between the partisans of "prickles" and the partisans of "goo." The prickly people are tough-minded, rigorous, and precise, and like to stress differences and divisions between things. They prefer particles to waves, and discontinuity to continuity. The gooey people are tender-minded romanticists who love wide generalizations and grand syntheses. They stress the underlying unities, and are inclined to pantheism and mysticism. Waves suit them much better than particles as the ultimate constituents of matter, and discontinuities jar their teeth like a compressed-air drill. Prickly philosophers consider the gooey ones rather disgusting—undisciplined, vague dreamers who slide over hard facts like an intellectual slime which threatens to engulf the whole universe in an "undifferentiated aesthetic continuum" (courtesy of Professor F. S. C. Northrop). But gooey philosophers think of their prickly colleagues as animated skeletons that rattle and click without any flesh or vital juices, as dry and dessicated mechanisms bereft of all finer feelings. Either party would be hopelessly lost without the other, because there would be nothing to argue about, no one would know what his position was, and the whole course of philosophy would come to an end.

As things now stand in the world of academic philosophy, the prickly people have had the upper hand in both England and the United States for some years. With their penchant for linguistic analysis, mathematical logic, and scientific empiricism, they have aligned philosophy with the mystique of science, have begun to transform the philosopher's library or mountain retreat into something nearer to a laboratory, and, as William Earle said, would come to work in white coats if they thought they could get away with it. The professional journals are now as satisfactorily unreadable as treatises on mathematical physics, and the points at issue as minute as any animalcule in the biologist's microscope. But their sweeping victory over the gooey people has almost abolished philosophy as a discipline, for we are close to the point where departments of philosophy will close their offices and shift the remaining members of their faculties to the departments of mathematics and linguistics.

Historically, this is probably the extreme point of that swing of the intellectual pendulum which brought into fashion the Fully Automatic Model of the universe, of the age of analysis and specialization when we lost our vision of the universe in the overwhelming complexity of its details.[3] But by a process which C. G. Jung called

[3]Academic philosophy missed its golden opportunity in 1921, when Ludwig Wittgenstein first published his *Tractatus Logico-Philosophicus,* which ended with the following passage: "The right method of philosophy would be this. To say nothing except what can be said, *i.e.* the propositions of natural science, *i.e.* something that has nothing to do with philosophy: and then always, when someone else wished to say something metaphysical, to demonstrate to him that he had given no meaning to certain signs in his propositions. This method would be unsatisfying to the other—he would not have the feeling that we were teaching him philosophy—but it would be the only strictly correct method. My propositions are elucidatory in this way: he who understands me finally recognizes them as senseless, when he has climbed out through them, on them, over them. (He must so to speak throw away the ladder, after he has climbed up on it.) He must surmount these

"enantiodromia," the attainment of any extreme position is the point where it begins to turn into its own
opposite—a process that can be dreary and repetitious
without the realization that opposite extremes are polar,
and that poles need each other. There are no prickles
without goo, and no goo without prickles.

To go anywhere in philosophy, other than back and
forth, round and round, one must have a keen sense of
correlative vision. This is a technical term for a thorough
understanding of the Game of Black-and-White,
whereby one sees that all explicit opposites are implicit
allies—correlative in the sense that they "gowith" each
other and cannot exist apart. This, rather than any mi-
asmic absorption of differences into a continuum of ultimate goo, is the metaphysical unity underlying the
world. For this unity is not mere one-ness as opposed
to multiplicity, since these two terms are themselves
polar. The unity, or inseparability, of one and many is
therefore referred to in Vedanta philosophy as "non-
duality" *(advaita)* to distinguish it from simple unifor-
mity. True, the term has its own opposite, "duality,"
for insofar as every term designates a class, an intellectual pigeonhole, every class has an outside polarizing its

propositions; then he sees the world rightly. Whereof one cannot
speak, thereof one must be silent." This was the critical moment
for all academic philosophers to maintain total silence and to ad-
vance the discipline to the level of pure contemplation along the
lines of the meditation practices of the Zen Buddhists. But even
Wittgenstein had to go on talking and writing, for how else can a
philosopher show that he is working and not just goofing off? (The
above passage is from the English translation of the *Tractatus,* published by Routledge & Kegan Paul, London, 1929. Sections 6.53,
6.54, and 7, pp. 187–89.)

inside. For this reason, language can no more transcend duality than paintings or photographs upon a flat surface can go beyond two dimensions. Yet by the convention of perspective, certain two-dimensional lines that slant towards a "vanishing-point" are taken to represent the third dimension of depth. In a similar way, the dualistic term "non-duality" is taken to represent the "dimension" in which explicit differences have implicit unity.

It is not at first easy to maintain correlative vision. The *Upanishads* describe it as the path of the razor's edge, a balancing act on the sharpest and thinnest of lines. For to ordinary vision there is nothing visible "between" classes and opposites. Life is a series of urgent choices demanding firm commitment to this or to that. Matter is as much like something as something can be, and space is as much like nothing as nothing can be. Any common dimension between them seems inconceivable, unless it is our own consciousness or mind, and this doubtless belongs to the side of matter— everlastingly threatened by nothingness. Yet with a slight shift of viewpoint, nothing is more obvious than the interdependence of opposites. But who can believe it?

Is it possible that myself, my existence, so *contains* being and nothing that death is merely the "off" interval in an on/off pulsation which must be eternal—because every alternative to this pulsation (e.g., its absence) would in due course imply its presence? Is it conceivable, then, that I am basically an eternal existence momentarily and perhaps needlessly terrified by one half of itself because it has identified all of itself with the other half? If the choice must be either white or black, must I so commit myself to the white side that I cannot be a good sport and actually play the Game of Black-and-White, with the implicit knowledge that neither can win? Or is all this so much bandying with the formal relations between words and terms without any relation to my physical situation?

To answer the last question affirmatively, I should have to believe that the logic of thought is quite arbitrary—that it is a purely and strictly human invention without any basis in the physical universe. While it is true, as I have already shown, that we do project logical patterns (nets, grids, and other types of calculus) upon the wiggly physical world—which can be confusing if we do not realize what we are doing—nevertheless, these patterns do not come from *outside* the world. They have something to do with the design of the human nervous system, which is definitely in and of the world. Furthermore, I have shown that correlative thinking about the relation of organism to environment is far more compatible with the physical sciences than our archaic and prevalent notions of the self as something confronting an alien and separate world. To sever the connections between human logic and the physical universe, I would have to revert to the myth of the ego as an isolated, independent observer for whom the rest of the world is absolutely external and "other." Neither neurology nor biology nor sociology can subscribe to this.

If, on the other hand, self and other, subject and object, organism and environment are the poles of a single process, THAT is my true existence. As the *Upanishads* say, "That is the Self. That is the real. That art thou!"

But I cannot think or say anything about THAT, or, as I shall now call it, IT, unless I resort to the convention of using dualistic language as the lines of perspective are used to show depth on a flat surface. What lies beyond opposites must be discussed, if at all, in terms of opposites, and this means using the language of analogy, metaphor, and myth.

The difficulty is not only that language is dualistic, insofar as words are labels for mutually exclusive classes. The problem is that IT is so much more myself than I thought I was, so central and so basic to my existence, that I cannot make it an object. There is no way to stand outside IT, and, in fact, no need to do so. For so long as I am trying to grasp IT, I am implying that IT is not really myself. If it were possible, I am losing the sense of it by attempting to find it. This is why those who really know that they are IT invariably say they do not understand it, for IT understands understanding—not the other way about. One cannot, and need not, go deeper than deep!

But the fact that IT eludes every description must not, as happens so often, be mistaken for the description of IT as the airiest of abstractions, as a literal transparent continuum or undifferentiated cosmic jello. The most concrete image of God the Father, with his white beard and golden robe, is better than that. Yet Western students of Eastern philosophies and religions persistently accuse Hindus and Buddhists of believing in a featureless and gelatinous God, just because the latter insist that every conception or objective image of IT is void. But the term "void" applies to all such conceptions, not to IT.

Yet in speaking and thinking of IT, there is no alternative to the use of conceptions and images, and no harm in it so long as we realize what we are doing. Idolatry is not the use of images, but confusing them with what they represent, and in this respect mental images and lofty abstractions can be more insidious than bronze idols.

You were probably brought up in a culture where the presiding image of IT has for centuries been God the Father, whose pronoun is He, because IT seems too impersonal and She would, of course, be inferior. Is this image still workable, as a functional myth to provide some consensus about life and its meaning for all the diverse peoples and cultures of this planet?

Frankly, the image of God the Father has become ridiculous—that is, unless you read Saint Thomas Aquinas or Martin Buber or Paul Tillich, and realize that you can be a devout Jew or Christian without having to believe, literally, in the Cosmic Male Parent. Even then, it is difficult not to feel the force of the image, because images sway our emotions more deeply than conceptions. As a devout Christian you would be saying day after day the prayer, "Our Father who art in heaven," and eventually it gets you: you are relating emotionally to IT as to an idealized father—male, loving but stern, and a personal being quite other than yourself. Obviously, you must be other than God so long as you conceive yourself as the separate ego, but when we realize that this form of identity is no more than a social institution, and one which has ceased to be a workable life-game, the sharp division between oneself and the ultimate reality is no longer relevant.

Furthermore, the younger members of our society

have for some time been in growing rebellion against paternal authority and the paternal state. For one reason, the home in an industrial society is chiefly a dormitory, and the father does not work there, with the result that wife and children have no part in his vocation. He is just a character who brings in money, and after working hours he is supposed to forget about his job and have fun. Novels, magazines, television, and popular cartoons therefore portray "Dad" as an incompetent clown. And the image has some truth in it because Dad has fallen for the hoax that work is simply something you do to make money, and with money you can get anything you want.

It is no wonder that an increasing proportion of college students want no part in Dad's world, and will do anything to avoid the rat-race of the salesman, commuter, clerk, and corporate executive. Professional men, too—architects, doctors, lawyers, ministers, and professors—have offices away from home, and thus, because the demands of their families boil down more and more to money, are ever more tempted to regard even professional vocations as ways of making money. All this is further aggravated by the fact that parents no longer educate their own children. Thus the child does not grow up with understanding of or enthusiasm for his father's work. Instead, he is sent to an understaffed school run mostly by women which, under the circumstances, can do no more than hand out mass–produced education which prepares the child for everything and nothing. It has no relation whatever to his father's vocation.

Along with this devaluation of the father, we are becoming accustomed to a conception of the universe so mysterious and so impressive that even the best father-image will no longer do for an explanation of what makes it run. But the problem then is that it is impossible for us to conceive an image higher than the human image. Few of us have ever met an angel, and probably would not recognize it if we saw one, and our images of an impersonal or suprapersonal God are hopelessly subhuman—jello, featureless light, homogenized space, or a whopping jolt of electricity. However, our image of man is changing as it becomes clearer and clearer that the human being is not simply and only his physical organism. My body is also my total environment, and this must be measured by light-years in the billions.

Hitherto the poets and philosophers of science have used the vast expanse and duration of the universe as a pretext for reflections on the unimportance of man, forgetting that man with "that enchanted loom, the brain" is precisely what transforms this immense electrical pulsation into light and color, shape and sound, large and small, hard and heavy, long and short. In knowing the world we humanize it, and if, as we discover it, we are astonished at its dimensions and its complexity, we should be just as astonished that we have the brains to perceive it.

Hitherto we have been taught, however, that we are not really responsible for our brains. We do not know (in terms of words or figures) how they are constructed, and thus it seems that the brain and the organism as a whole are an ingenious vehicle which has been "given" to us, or an uncanny maze in which we are temporarily trapped. In other words, we accepted a definition of ourselves which confined the self to the source and to the limitations of conscious attention. This definition is miserably insufficient, for in fact we know how to grow brains and eyes, ears and fingers, hearts and bones, in just the same way that we know how to walk and breathe, talk and think—only we can't put it into words. Words are too slow and too clumsy for describing such things, and conscious attention is too narrow for keeping track of all their details.

Thus it will often happen that when you tell a girl how beautiful she is, she will say, "Now isn't that just like a man! All you men think about is bodies. OK, so I'm beautiful, but I got my body from my parents and it was just luck. I prefer to be admired for myself, not my chassis." Poor little chauffeur! All she is saying is that she has lost touch with her own astonishing wisdom and ingenuity, and wants to be admired for some trivial tricks that she can perform with her conscious attention. And we are all in the same situation, having dissociated ourselves from our bodies and from the whole network of forces in which bodies can come to birth and live.

Yet we can still awaken the sense that all this, too, is the self—a self, however, which is far beyond the image of the ego, or of the human body as limited by the skin. We then behold the Self wherever we look, and its image is the universe in its light and in its darkness, in its bodies and in its spaces. This is the new image of man, but it is still an image. For there remains—to use dualistic words—"behind," "under," "encompassing," and "central" to it all the unthinkable IT, polarizing itself in the visible contrasts of waves and troughs, solids and spaces. But the odd thing is that this IT, however inconceivable, is no vapid abstraction: it is very simply and truly yourself.

In the words of a Chinese Zen master, "Nothing is left to you at this moment but to have a good laugh!" As James Broughton put it:

> *This is It*
> *and I am It*
> *and You are It*
> *and so is That*
> *and He is It*
> *and She is It*
> *and It is It*
> *and That is That.*[4]

True humor is, indeed, laughter at one's Self—at the Divine Comedy, the fabulous deception, whereby one comes to imagine that a creature *in* existence is not also *of* existence, that what man is is not also what everything is. All the time we "know it in our bones" but conscious attention, distracted by details and differences, cannot see the whole for the parts.

The major trick in this deception is, of course, death. Consider death as the permanent end of consciousness, the point at which you and your knowledge of the universe simply cease, and where you become as if you had never existed at all. Consider it also on a much vaster scale—the death of the universe at the time when

[4]From *The Bard and the Harper,* recorded by James Broughton and Joel Andrews. LP-1013, produced by Musical Engineering Associates, Sausalito, California, 1965.

all energy runs out, when, according to some cosmologists, the explosion which flung the galaxies into space fades out like a skyrocket. It will be as if it had never happened, which is, of course, the way things were before it *did* happen. Likewise, when you are dead, you will be as you were before you were conceived. So—there has been a flash, a flash of consciousness or a flash of galaxies. It happened. Even if there is no one left to remember.

But if, when it has happened and vanished, things are at all as they were before it began (including the possibility that there were no things), it can happen again. Why not? On the other hand, I might suppose that after it has happened things aren't the same as they were before. Energy was present before the explosion, but after the explosion died out, no energy was left. For ever and ever energy was latent. Then it blew up, and that was that. It is, perhaps, possible to imagine that what had always existed got tired of itself, blew up, and stopped. But this is a greater strain on my imagination than the idea that these flashes are periodic and rhythmic. They may go on and on, or round and round: it doesn't make much difference. Furthermore, if latent energy had *always* existed before the explosion, I find it difficult to think of a single, particular time coming when it had to stop. Can anything be half eternal? That is, can a process which had no beginning come to an end?

I presume, then, that with my own death I shall forget who I was, just as my conscious attention is unable to recall, if it ever knew, how to form the cells of the brain and the pattern of the veins. Conscious memory plays little part in our biological existence. Thus as my sensation of "I-ness," of being alive, once came into being without conscious memory or intent, so it will arise again and again, as the "central" Self—the IT— appears as the self/other situation in its myriads of pulsating forms—always the same and always new, a here in the midst of a there, a now in the midst of then, and a one in the midst of many. And if I forget how many times I have been here, and in how many shapes, this forgetting is the necessary interval of darkness between every pulsation of light. I return in every baby born.

Actually, we know this already. After people die, babies are born—and, unless they are automata, every one of them is, just as we ourselves were, the "I" experience coming again into being. The conditions of heredity and environment change, but each of those babies incarnates the same experience of being central to a world that is "other." Each infant dawns into life as I did, without any memory of a past. Thus when I am gone there can be no experience, no living through, of the state of being a perpetual "has-been." Nature "abhors the vacuum" and the I-feeling appears again as it did before, and it matters not whether the interval be ten seconds or billions of years. In unconsciousness all times are the same brief instant.

This is so obvious, but our block against seeing it is the ingrained and compelling myth that the "I" comes into this world, or is thrown out from it, in such a way as to have no essential connection with it. Thus we do not trust the universe to repeat what it has already done—to "I" itself again and again. We see it as an eternal arena in which the individual is no more than a temporary stranger—a visitor who hardly belongs—for the thin ray of consciousness does not shine upon its own source. In looking out upon the world, we forget that the world is looking at itself—through our eyes and IT's.

Now you know—even if it takes you some time to do a double-take and get the full impact. It may not be easy to recover from the many generations through which the fathers have knocked down the children, like dominoes, saying, "Don't you dare think that thought! You're just a little upstart, just a creature, and you had better learn your place." On the contrary, you're IT. But perhaps the fathers were unwittingly trying to tell the children that IT plays IT cool. You don't come on (that is, on stage) like IT because you really are IT, and the point of the stage is to show on, not to show off. To come on like IT—to play at being God—is to play the Self as a role, which is just what it isn't. When IT plays, it plays at being everything else.

THE BOOKS

These are books which, from many differing points of view, bear upon and expand the themes of *The Book*.

Reginald H. Blyth, *Zen in English Literature and Oriental Classics*. Dutton, New York, 1960.

Norman O. Brown, *Life Against Death: The Psychoanalytical Meaning of History*. Wesleyan University Press, Middletown, Conn., 1959.

Richard M. Bucke, *Cosmic Consciousness*. Rev. ed. Dutton, New York, 1959.

Trigant Burrow, *Science and Man's Behavior*. Philosophical Library, New York, 1958.

Wing-tsit Chan, *The Platform Scripture of the Sixth Patriarch*. St. John's University Press, New York, n.d.

S. P. R. Charter, *Man on Earth: A Preliminary Evaluation of the Ecology of Man.* Contact Editions, The Tides, Sausalito, Cal., 1962.

Alexandra David-Neel, *The Secret Oral Teachings in the Tibetan Buddhist Sects.* Maha-Bodhi Society, Calcutta, n.d.

Pierre Teilhard de Chardin, *The Phenomenon of Man.* Harper & Row, New York, 1959.

John Dewey and Arthur F. Bentley, *Knowing and the Known.* Beacon Press, Boston, 1960.

Georg Groddeck, *The Book of the It.* Vintage Books, New York, 1961.

René Guénon, *Introduction to the Study of the Hindu Doctrines.* Luzac, London, 1945.

Aldous Huxley, *Island.* Harper & Row, New York, 1962.

William James, *The Varieties of Religious Experience.* Modern Library, New York, 1936.

Raynor Carey Johnson, *Watcher on the Hills.* Harper & Row, New York, 1959.

Carl G. Jung, *Memories, Dreams, Reflections.* Recorded and edited by Aniela Jaffé. Pantheon, New York, 1963.

J. Krishnamurti, *Commentaries on Living.* 3 vols. Harper & Row, New York, 1956–60.

Lin Yutang, *The Wisdom of Lao-tse.* Modern Library, New York, 1948.

Sarvepalli Radhakrishnan, trans., *The Bhagavad-Gita.* Harper, New York, 1948.

——— , trans., *The Principal Upanishads.* Harper, New York, 1953.

D. T. Suzuki, *Zen Buddhism.* Ed. William Barrett. Doubleday, New York, 1956.

Alan Watts, *Nature, Man, and Woman*. Pantheon, New York, 1958.

Raymond H. Wheeler, *The Laws of Human Nature*. Nisbet, London, 1931.

Lancelot Law Whyte, *The Next Development in Man*. Holt, New York, 1948.

Richard Wilhelm and Carl G. Jung, *The Secret of the Golden Flower*. Harcourt, Brace, New York, 1962.

Ludwig Wittgenstein, *Tractatus Logico-Philosophicus*. Routledge and Kegan Paul, London, and Humanities Press, New York, 1961.

John Z. Young, *Doubt and Certainty in Science*. Oxford University Press, New York, 1960.

About the Author

ALAN WATTS, who held both a master's degree in theology and a doctorate of divinity, has earned the reputation of being one of the most original and
"unrutted" philosophers of the century. He is best
known as an interpreter of Zen Buddhism in particular,
and of Indian and Chinese philosophy in general. He
was the author of more than twenty books on the philosophy and psychology of religion, including (in Vintage Books) *Behold the Spirit, Does It Matter? The Joyous
Cosmology, Nature, Man and Woman, The Supreme Identity, The Way of Zen, The Wisdom of Insecurity, This Is It,
Beyond Theology, Psychotherapy East and West,* and *Cloud-
Hidden, Whereabouts Unknown: A Mountain Journal.* He
died in 1973.

Also by

ALAN WATTS

A journal for practical wisdom and self-reflection—featuring insightful quotes, sage advice for a life well lived, and charming illustrations from acclaimed philosopher Alan Watts. Whether you are familiar with his work or new to it, these inspiring messages will guide you in the mindful practice of journaling.

AVAILABLE EXCLUSIVELY IN HARDCOVER

Learn more at knopfdoubleday.com